Driving the Great Western Trail in Arizona

An Off-road Travel Guide to the Great Western Trail in Arizona

by

Raymond C. Andrews
and
Jennifer L Andrews

BOOKS BY RAYMOND C. ANDREWS, M.D.

Medical Grail

The Life and Times of Benjamin Wiggins, M.D.

How to Be a Patient and Live to Tell the Tale!

Driving the Great Western Trail in Arizona

Majette Publications First Edition 2011

Copyright © 2011 Raymond C. Andrews

Illustrations © 2011 Raymond C. Andrews

Photographs © 2011 Raymond C. Andrews and Jennifer L. Andrews

Website: www.medicalgrail.com

Email: majettebooks@cox.net

ISBN-13: 978-1456568030

ISBN-10: 1456568035

Acknowledgments

We would like to thank the many dedicated Forest Rangers in the state of Arizona whose friendly help and invaluable information made this book possible.

We would also like to thank Tracey Hackworth for permission to reprint Tread Lightly!'s logo and "Quick Tips for Responsible Driving" in its entirety.

Disclaimer

Although we have made every attempt to ensure the accuracy of the information herein, we and the publisher disclaim any and all liability for any loss, inconvenience, vehicle damage or personal injury that may occur to anyone who uses this guidebook.

Driving the Great Western Trail in Arizona is not a survival manual. Off-road travel always presents risks, and the mere fact that a trail or road has been described in this guidebook does not mean it will be safe for you to travel on it.

Road conditions will change after floods, landslides, and other natural disasters, and you may encounter obstacles far worse than what are described in this book. It is therefore incumbent upon you to check road conditions and to know your vehicle's limitations before attempting to drive any of these trails.

We have written *Driving the Great Western Trail in Arizona* to help you enjoy the splendor of Arizona's backcountry. Although you can drive some sections of the trail in a passenger car, we assume you are an experienced off-road driver and will be driving a high-clearance 4-wheel drive vehicle that is properly maintained and equipped for travel on unmaintained, unpaved, primitive, and remote roads and trails.

Driving the Great Western Trail in Arizona is not an instruction manual for off-road driving, since experience driving on primitive roads can come only through practice under the guidance of an expert. Nor is it intended to be the sole source of information regarding the Great Western Trail. Some maps and other information are available at no charge from the Ranger Stations in the various Forest Districts.

Be safe! Exercise caution, bring proper supplies and be ready to treat injuries and to repair vehicle breakdowns yourself. It may be a long time before help reaches you on the more remote trails.

Rock Formation along Highway 89

Once upon a time in the West

In 1776, while states on America's east coast were declaring independence from England, two Spanish priests, Dominguez and Escalante, were camping with Paiute Indians at the base of the Kaibab Plateau in northern Arizona. The trail the Indians showed them, the Jacob Hamblin/Mormon Honeymoon Trail, still exists, as do the Beale Wagon Road and the Moqui Stage Station. Today's adventurers can travel these trails and visit these sites on All Terrain Vehicles (ATVs), bicycles, horseback, snowmobiles, or as we do in a modified Jeep towing an off-road trailer.

These trails welcome those yearning to follow in their ancestors' wagon ruts, and except for the fires, floods, and landslides that have occurred over the past centuries, they remain as they were when pioneers, cattle ranchers, and Mormon Honeymooners first ventured into Arizona: teeming with wildlife, exotic plants, and breathtaking rock formations that expose the history of the earth.

Driving the Great Western Trail in Arizona will help you drive the trail from Phoenix to the Utah border on some of the same roads your ancestors traveled 200 years ago. The Trail is long and lonely, and days without Face Book and Twitter can lead to erratic and sometimes violent behavior, yet if you are willing to leave civilization behind, driving through Arizona's spectacular backcountry is an experience you will not forget.

Book Contents

Chapter One:
History of the Great Western Trail

The Great Western Trail was conceived in the 1980s as a 4,500-mile long network of preexisting trails that would traverse a broad corridor through central Arizona, Utah, and Wyoming, and end at the Idaho-Montana border with Canada. It was designed to serve all-terrain vehicles, 4x4 enthusiasts, motorcyclists, horseback riders, hikers, and in the high country, snowmobile riders. It derives its name from the joining of the Arizona and Bonneville Rim Trails.

In Arizona the Trail with its "Points of Discovery" historic and instructive sites, is over 350 miles long. It begins in Phoenix in the southern Basin and Range (desert) Region where vegetation is sparse, but cacti, mixed grasses, chaparral, and sagebrush thrive in the alkali soil. Next it travels through the Central Highlands (mountainous) Region in the middle of the state. Here, with elevations between 5,000 and 10,000 feet, temperatures remain high throughout the year, and piñon trees, Apache fir, aspen, and bristlecone pine abound.

It ends in the northern Colorado Plateau Region with tablelands ranging from 5,000 to 7,000 feet. Winters are cold, but summers are warm. Rain is common, and Douglas fir and Ponderosa pine grow in the Kaibab National Forest and on these high plateaus.

The first leg of the trail, Bulldog Canyon in the Tonto National Forest, was dedicated in April 1996. Two years later the Cave Creek segment and the Sears-Kay Ruin were added. This trail passes the Seven Springs Campground, an oasis developed by the Civilian Conservation Corps almost 100 years ago, as it winds its way to Bloody Basin Road.

From here you can drive through the Agua Fria National Monument to I-17 or turn north on a rocky trail that crosses shale ledges and rivers to Dugas and then to the San Dominique Winery before it crosses Interstate 17.

The Trail continues across I-17, winding its way through grass-lands, across riverbeds, and over Mingus Mountain, to Highway 89A where it enters the Martin Canyon, also known as Smiley Rock because of a pumpkin sized rock on the side of the trail that has eyes, nose, and a mouth.

From here it is a leisurely ride to Jerome, a mining town that became a ghost town half a century ago, and which, according to local lore, is still inhabited by specters. Artisans have revived it and it is now a well-known tourist destination. The town sits on unstable ground and is in constant downhill motion as astute visitors may notice from necklaces that swing almost imperceptibly on their stands in jewelry store display cases.

After Jerome the trail goes north to Perkinsville in the Verde Valley, then onto the Mogollon Rim and White Horse Lake where the temperature is noticeably cooler. Nearby Sycamore Canyon with its red sandstone sculptures is an unsung treasure and you should not miss it.

The trail continues through forests and prairies to Parks and Williams, where you will find food, lodging, and gasoline. It is less challenging as it continues north of Parks though the grasslands and forests of the Williams Ranger District of the Kaibab National Forest, until it enters the Tusayan Ranger District and then the Navajo Reservation. Here, after finding your way through a bewildering patchwork of unmarked paths, you will get a spectacular view of the Little Colorado River Gorge as you descend to Highway 64.

The trail ends here before restarting at House Rock on Highway 89A, but before driving into the mountains, stop at the Navajo Tribal Park Ranger Station at the junction of Highways 89 and 64 to pick up a permit to camp on the reservation near the Hopi Salt Trail. In n Cameron you can also get supplies, a mouthwatering Navajo Taco, and Native American jewelry and pottery.

Continuing north on Highway 89 on your way to the last legs of the trail, you will cross Marble Canyon Gorge on the Navajo Bridge and then flank the Vermilion Cliffs. The views along this highway of Echo Cliffs and the green, gray, blue, and lavender hills of Chinle Formation are spectacular.

The trail starts again at House Rock with a difficult ascent into the mountains along a trail that skirts the base of the Kaibab Plateau. A marker states that Spanish priests Dominquez and Escalante traded for food with the Paiute Indians in 1776.

The last leg, from Jacob Lake to Utah with its breath-taking view of the Chocolate, Vermilion, and White Cliffs, may be the most scenic.

The Great Western Trail is a long route without water, fuel, or fast-food restaurants along the way. It will challenge the most adventurous, and will enlighten and amaze those searching for a return to a primitive and exciting respite from the hustle and bustle of civilization.

Arizona wildlife is abundant along this trail, and you are likely to see Rocky Mountain elk, white-tailed and mule deer, horses, antelope, black bear, and many others. Contrary to picture-postcards sold in many tourist stops, however, the jackalope, a jackrabbit with antelope horns, is not native to the state.

Pause along Highway 89A near Marble Canyon

Chapter Two:
Safety & Rules of the Road

The Great Western Trail is exciting, informative, and challenging, but it can also be unforgiving. In its long trek from Phoenix to the Utah border, it meanders through sandy deserts and forested mountains. None is impossible, although each presents its own challenges requiring its own set of driving rules. Even so, motor sports and especially off-road driving, are potentially dangerous. Be prepared and use good judgment when driving the trail.

It is not within the scope of our book to teach off-road driving, but we will describe some of the obstacles you may face and suggest how to overcome them. You can find more detailed instruction, including videos, at Tread Lightly!, www.treadlightly.org, and other online sites. If you have no experience in off-road travel, before driving these trails we suggest you take a course with a qualified instructor or join a 4-wheelers club and go on several trips with its members.

Know your vehicle and its capabilities

A skilled driver in a high clearance vehicle with 4-wheel drive should have no difficulty with any leg of the Great Western Trail, but an unskilled driver will, no matter how modified his vehicle may be. Unless someone has moved them since we wrote this book, wrecked vehicles along several of the trails bear silent witness to our warning. The specific cause of the accidents is unknown, but there are at least two reasons: the driver did not understand his abilities and the capabilities of his vehicle and drove both over their limits, or his vehicle had problems that were unknown or not corrected before beginning the trip.

Make sure you or your local mechanic inspect your vehicle before you begin your trip. Top up all fluids, check for leaks, and make any necessary repairs. They are easier to make in a warm, dry garage than on the side of a mountain during a blizzard.

Travel alone or in company

There is no easy answer to this question. Some people suggest you always travel with others since they will be there to help immediately in case of an accident or breakdown. It may be wise to travel in a group of at least two vehicles if the trail is remote and challenging, as parts of the Great Western Trail are.

Others feel that if you drive a well-maintained SUV, are experienced in off-road driving techniques, and have a communications device that is more effective in remote areas than a cellphone (such as a satellite phone or a Personal Locator Beacon), it is safe to travel alone.

Know where you're going

The maps and waypoint coordinates in this book will help you find your way through each leg of the Great Western Trail, and you should study them carefully before beginning your journey. To use the coordinates, you will need a good GPS unit, possibly with a remote antenna, or a laptop computer with topographic software, such as Fugawi or Terrain Navigator, and a GPS receiver.

You should have maps of the national forests, which you can purchase from the USDA Forest Service at www.nationalforeststore.-com. You can also find maps of the GWT at Ranger Stations in the Tonto, Prescott, and Kaibab National Forests. These are free but limited in scope and contain errors which we have pointed out in this book.

Before starting your trip, you should know where each trail begins and ends as well as its length and any obstacles it may present. Note the location of nearby towns in case you need supplies or assistance, as there are no stores or service stations along the trails. And before you go, especially if you go alone, tell someone where you will be and how long you expect to be away. Cellphone service is erratic or nonexistent on most of the trails.

Know the weather

The number one cause of death from natural phenomena in Arizona is flash floods, and you can find yourself in a torrent of water even if it is not raining where you are. This happens regularly in the

Grand Canyon. Do not travel these trails when heavy rains are predicted in the area. A dry wash that was a perfect area to set up your tent can turn into a river overnight, sweeping you and all your equipment downstream in minutes.

Necessary Equipment

We offer a list of suggested items to bring with you in Appendix A. Bring only what you think you will need. Spare axles and transfer cases, even if some off-road magazines suggest them, are generally not necessary and their weight will change your spry Jeep into an unwieldy tank.

Driving obstacles along the Great Western Trail

Driving in the desert

The trails around Phoenix are all in a desert environment and are heavily traveled, especially on weekends and holidays. As a result the sand is well packed and will present few challenges. However the spines from the cacti, trees and bushes that line these trails may. If your vehicle breaks down, or if you get a flat from a spine and do not have a spare or puncture repair kit (I know a driver who leaves his spare at home because he gets better mileage without it), stay near your vehicle unless you know how far you are from the nearest source of aid. Your supplies and shade are in your vehicle, and rescuers can more easily spot a large vehicle in the middle of a known trail than a dehydrated body under a bush.

Make shade from whatever you have available to protect you from the sun. Keep your clothes on, wear a head covering, and do not sit on the ground. It will be much hotter than the air.

Driving on sand

Fine sand, as you will find in the summer when it is extremely dry, is difficult to drive on and is best tackled in a 4-wheel drive vehicle in low gear with its tires aired down to 20 psi or less. Narrow tires will dig into the sand but flotation tires with their wide footprint, will be less likely to do so.

If your tires start spinning, get off the gas immediately so you do not dig yourself into the sand. If you do need to dig yourself out, put wood, rocks, or even your floor mats under your wheels for traction.

Avoid rocks in the sand. Like icebergs, they could be larger than you think and may damage your tires.

Drive as straight as possible since the front tires will pack down the sand making travel easier for the rear tires. Steering and breaking will take longer than usual, so plan for them in advance. If you need to park, try to park on a downhill slope.

Driving on gravel

Traction is less on gravel than on a paved road. Slow down when changing from one surface to another and leave plenty of distance between you and the vehicle you are following to avoid having your windshield cracked by flying rocks.

Driving over rocks

There are no large boulders on the trail, but there are small ones and ledges to climb over: use low gear, 4-wheel drive, and keep your speed at 1-3 mph.

Also lower your tire pressure and drive over the obstacles. Do not straddle rocks since you risk "high-centering" your vehicle. Cross ditches at an angle, one wheel at a time.

Driving over hills

If you cannot see over them, walk them first to see what is on the other side. Blasting over the top of a hill only to see the road curve sharply to the right as your vehicle careens off a cliff will ruin your trip.

Always drive straight up and down a hill, as turning on it may cause your vehicle to slide or to roll over. Increase power during the climb, but ease off the accelerator as you near the top of the hill. If your wheels spin, turning your steering wheel back and forth rapidly may help you regain traction.

If you stall on the way up, back straight down in reverse gear and use engine compression, not your brakes ,to slow your vehicle. 4-wheel drive and low gear is best in this situation.

Driving in mud

This is not a major problem on the GWT since there are bypasses around known trouble spots. Avoid it when you can, since unless you probe it, you have no idea how deep it is.

If you cannot avoid it, air down and switch into 4-WD low, third or fourth gear. Pick a line that looks shallow and dry before entering it. Drive fast enough to maintain momentum, but if your wheels start to spin, stop. As on a hill climb, turning your steering wheel back and forth rapidly may help you regain traction. If you get stuck, try backing out, again turning your steering wheel back and forth.

If you remain mired, you will have to dig your way out. Put rocks and whatever is handy under the tires. Jacking up your vehicle may be difficult if the mud is soupy for obvious reasons.

Rules of the Road

The following is reprinted with kind permission from Tracy Hackworth at Tread Lightly!, a nonprofit organization whose mission is "to promote responsible outdoor recreation through ethics education and stewardship."

We are responsible for keeping these trails open for the enjoyment of our children and grandchildren. The principles here, if followed by all of us, will ensure they will be.

Tread Lightly!'s website, www.treadlightly.org/ is a gold mine of information regarding all aspects of off-road travel and merits a visit.

TRAVEL RESPONSIBLY
Travel responsibly on designated roads, trails or areas.
- Travel only in areas open to four-wheel drive vehicles.
- For your safety, travel straight up or down hills.
- Drive over, not around obstacles to avoid widening the trail.
- Straddle ruts, gullies, and washouts even if they are wider than your vehicle.
- Cross streams only at designated fording points, where the road crosses the stream.
- When possible, avoid mud. In soft terrain, go easy on the gas to avoid wheel spin, which can cause rutting.
- Don't turn around on narrow roads, steep terrain, or unstable ground. Back up until you find a safe place to turn around.
- Stop frequently and scout ahead on foot. To help with traction,

balance your load and lower tire pressure to where you see a bulge (typically not less than 20 pounds).

⚤ Know where the differential or the lowest point on your vehicle is. This will help in negotiating terrain and prevent vehicle damage resulting in oil and fluid spills on the trail.

⚤ Maintain a reasonable distance between vehicles.

⚤ Comply with all signs and respect barriers.

⚤ Travel with a group of two or more vehicles. Driving solo can leave you vulnerable if you have an accident or breakdown. Designate meeting areas in case of separation.

⚤ Choose the appropriate winch for your vehicle size.

⚤ Attach towing cable, tree strap, or chain as low as possible to the object being winched. Let the winch do the work; never drive the winch.

⚤ When winching always inspect your equipment, use the right winch for the situation, find a good secure anchor, and never winch with less than five wraps of wire rope around the drum.

⚤ When using a tree as an anchor, use a wide tree strap to avoid damaging the trunk of the tree.

⚤ Don't mix driving with alcohol or drugs.

RESPECT THE RIGHTS OF OTHERS

Respect the rights of others, including private property owners, all recreational trail users, campers and others so they can enjoy their recreational activities undisturbed.

⚤ Be considerate of others on the road or trail.

⚤ Leave gates as you find them. If crossing private property, be sure to ask permission from the landowner(s).

⚤ Yield the right of way to those passing you traveling uphill. Yield to mountain bikers, hikers, and horses.

⚤ When encountering horses on the trail, move to the side of the trail, stop, turn off your engine, and speak – you want the horse to know you are human. Ask the rider the best way to proceed.

⚤ Proceed with caution around horses and pack animals. Sudden, unfamiliar activity may spook animals – possibly causing injury to animals, handlers, and others on the trail.

⚤ Do not idly ride around in camping, picnicking, trailhead, or residential areas.

⚘ Keep speeds low around crowds and in camping areas.

⚘ Keep the noise and dust down.

EDUCATE YOURSELF

Educate yourself prior to your trip by obtaining travel maps and regulations from public agencies, planning for your trip, taking recreation skills classes, and knowing how to operate your equipment safely.

⚘ Obtain a map - motor vehicle use map where appropriate - of your destination and determine which areas are open to off-highway vehicles.

⚘ Make a realistic plan and stick to it. Always tell someone of your travel plans.

⚘ Contact the land manager for area restrictions, closures, and permit requirements.

⚘ Check the weather forecast before you go. Prepare for the unexpected by packing necessary emergency items.

⚘ Buckle-up! Seat belts are mandatory. Know your limitations. Watch your time, your fuel, and your energy.

⚘ Take an off-highway drivers course to learn more about negotiating terrain in a four-wheel drive vehicle.

⚘ Make sure your vehicle is mechanically up to task. Be prepared with tools, supplies, spares, and a spill kit for trailside repairs.

AVOID SENSITIVE AREAS

Avoid sensitive areas such as meadows, lake shores, wetlands and streams. Stay on designated routes.

⚘ Other sensitive habitats to avoid include living desert soils, tundra, and seasonal nesting or breeding areas.

⚘ Do not disturb historical, archeological, or paleontological sites.

⚘ Avoid "spooking" livestock and wildlife you encounter and keep your distance.

⚘ Motorized and mechanized vehicles are not allowed in designated Wilderness Areas.

DO YOUR PART

Do your part by modeling appropriate behavior, leaving

the area better than you found it, properly disposing of waste, minimizing the use of fire, avoiding the spread of invasive species, and restoring degraded areas.

- Carry a trash bag on your vehicle and pick up litter left by others.
- Pack out what you pack in. Practice minimum impact camping by using established sites, camping 200 feet from water resources and trails.
- Observe proper sanitary waste disposal or pack your waste out.
- Protect the soundscape by preventing unnecessary noise created by a poorly tuned vehicle or revving your engine.
- Before and after a ride, wash your vehicle to reduce the spread of invasive species.
- Build a trail community. Get to know other types of recreationists that share your favorite trail.

Chapter Three:
How to Use This Guide

When we began writing this book, we wanted to include every-thing even minimally associated with the Great Western Trail. We soon realized that describing every rock formation, every plant, every animal, as well as every nearby city, town, or park, would result in an encyclopedia and not a guidebook.

The Great Western Trail is an adventure, and to experience it fully you must explore it, study it, and live it. As a result we chose to give you the important, difficult-to-find information about the trail and enough of its interesting geology, history, botany and zoology to stim-ulate you to research it before you set out. We have listed books and references that will help you in this task in the bibliography.

Trail Names
We assigned numbers to each of the trails for convenience only. Where they exist, we also used their official or semi-official names. For example, 4-wheelers know our Great Western Trail 7 as Smiley Rock. Maps refer to it as Martin Canyon. Others trails take their names from where they start and end, such as Great Western Trail 9: Interstate 40 to US 180.

Open Months/Best Time to Travel
The trails in the southern part of the state are open year-round, but because of the intense desert heat, it is better to travel them in the spring, fall, and winter.

In the northern part of the state, the trails may be closed from December to the middle of May because of snow or flooding. Official campsites are also closed during the winter months, but if the trails are open, dispersed camping is allowed. The nighttime temperatures in the desert can be 30 degrees colder than daytime temperatures, so bring warm clothing with you. A sleeping bag will come in handy if you break down along the trail and have to spend the night under the stars.

Rain is scarce until monsoon season but when it begins, roads become impassable and flash flooding occurs. Do not camp in washes and stay out of narrow canyons when rains are predicted.

Permits

At this time you need a permit drive on state lands, in the Tonto Forest, on Indian Lands, and to drive Bulldog Canyon. You can buy them in person, through the mail, or online. Addresses are listed in Appendix B. You may need other permits in the future, so check with the ranger stations before setting out.

Mileage

The mileage indicated for each trail is taken from tracks we recorded in Terrain Navigator Mapping Software using a Navibe GM720 receiver, and is presumed to be accurate. However the distance between waypoints is approximate. We made every effort to ensure accuracy, but many variables, from rerouting of the trails after flooding or rockslides, to GPS inaccuracy, to the tire size on your modified Jeep will cause minor discrepancies.

The waypoint coordinates are also approximate because of the inherent errors in the system. However they are on the tracks shown on our maps, and minor discrepancies should not cause difficulty.

Travel Time

We calculated time based one Jeep traveling non-stop along the trail at a safe speed. If you intend to travel in a group, picnic or camp along the way, or are in a hurry to complete the trail, your time will be longer or shorter than ours.

Difficulty is relative

The idea behind the creation of the Great Western Trail was to make it open to novice and expert drivers alike, and it is. But parts of it are dangerous if you do not have off-road driving experience. You can drive short sections of some of the trails in a Cadillac or Lincoln, but if you are not an experienced driver, you should avoid the three most difficult trails: Dugas (GWT 5), Smiley Rock (GWT 7), and the ascent from House Rock (GWT 11).

Driving skill, experience, and vehicle modification are different among those who will drive this trail, and what is difficult for you may not be for someone else. Before driving any of these trails, know and do not exceed your vehicle's limitations and your driving skills.

We base our ratings on the most difficult part of the trail. Therefore, if it is gravel for its entire length except for one obstacle you will need 4-WD and lockers to overcome, we rate the entire trail as difficult. Most trails are easy, which means they are gravel, washboard, or packed dirt and sand. We rate a trail as moderate when is it washed out, rutted, or rocky.

Remoteness

On a scale of 1 to 4, "1" suggests you will have company on the trail, especially on weekends and holidays. "4" suggests you will have only wildlife for company.

Services Available

There are no services along the trails. Most end or begin near a town or city where you can get food, supplies, and fuel, but some do not. Refuel before driving the longer trails, especially in the remote areas of northern Arizona.

Road Information and Restrictions

The Forest Rangers are your best source for up-to-date information about trail closures, changes, and seasonal restrictions, such as those regarding campfires. Floods, forest fires, and other natural disasters, may cause rerouting or even closure of a trail.

Arizona is known for its hot deserts, but it has a rainy season, and snow can be meters high in its northern region. At those times the forest roads are impassible. Check for restrictions and closures online or with the Rangers before setting out. Their addresses are in Appendix B.

General Permits

Before driving on any of the trails in this book, contact the ranger stations about permits. The information in this book was accurate at the time of its publication, but may change over time.

14

At this time you need a permit to camp or park in the recreation areas of the Tonto National Forest, but not to drive through it or to camp in non-recreational areas. You can buy it online, at many local stores or at ranger stations near the trails.

You will need a permit from the Arizona State Land Department to drive on State Trust Land. A downloadable pdf file, *Arizona Off-Highway Vehicle Guide, OHV Laws and Places to Ride,* gives valuable information about licensing regulations and other laws.

You will also need permits to drive the Bulldog Canyon in the Mesa District of the Tonto National Forest, and to drive or to camp on the Navajo Reservation.

You will find information at the ranger stations listed in Appendix B.

Camping Restrictions

The following information about dispersed camping comes from the US Department of the Interior Bureau of Land Management: http://www.blm.gov/ut/st/en/fo/st_george/recreation/camping/dispersed_camping.html

If you intend to camp along the GWT, please follow these regulations. Failure to do so could result in a forest fire or fine, or both.

It is the general policy of the BLM that undeveloped Federal lands under its administration are available to the public for camping and general recreation, with the following provisions:

- Camping at any one site is limited to 14 days per visit
- Pack out what you pack in
- Avoid camping within 200 ft. of any water source
- Do not leave campfires unattended.

Whenever camping outside designated campsites please practice the following minimum impact style camping:

Camp at previously used sites, if possible. Research studies have shown that the most rapid negative changes to soil and vegetation occur during the first few times a campsite is used.

Firepans or stoves are recommended when camping on BLM. A fire pan is a metal tray used to contain a campfire and prevent the fire from blackening the soil (oil pans work great!). Before breaking camp, it is a simple matter to transfer cold ashes into a plastic bag or other container for disposal at home. If you use a fire pan carefully, it is possible to leave a campsite with no scars or evidence of your use.

Avoid building new fire rings. Unnecessary fire rings scar the natural beauty of sites and reduce the amount of space available for sleeping and cooking areas.

Use only dead and down wood for campfires. Bringing your own firewood is the best policy to practice. Both dead and live trees add to the scenic qualities of campsites.

Do not put cans, bottles, or aluminum foil into a fire ring. These items do not burn, and their presence may lead subsequent users of the site to build a new fire ring.

Burn campfire logs to ashes, then douse with water. Do not smother a campfire with soil, as this will make it difficult for the next visitor to use the same fire ring. If you must leave a campsite before the fire burns all of the wood, douse the fire with water before you are ready to leave camp, then stir it with a stick, then douse it again to make sure it is completely out.

CAMPFIRES OF ANY KIND MAY BE BANNED DURING HIGH FIRE DANGER PERIODS.

Dispose of human waste properly. The use of portable toilets is highly recommended. If no portable toilet is available, solid body waste and urine should be buried in a hole six to twelve inches deep. The disposal site should be located well away from streams, campsite, and other use areas. Toilet paper should be placed in a small plastic bag and put into your camp trash bag.

Pack out your trash (and a little extra). Do not leave or bury trash at campsites. If you pack it in, pack it out.

Snow along Highway 180 near Great Western Trail 10

Road signs and their meanings

This is a primary route open to passenger cars, motor homes, and trailers.

This indicates the road is similar to a primary route but bumpier. As this sign has not as yet been universally adopted, it may sometimes indicate a high clearance road. Check with the Rangers before driving this trail if you have a low clearance vehicle.

Roads open to high clearance vehicles

Great Western Trail signs in Arizona

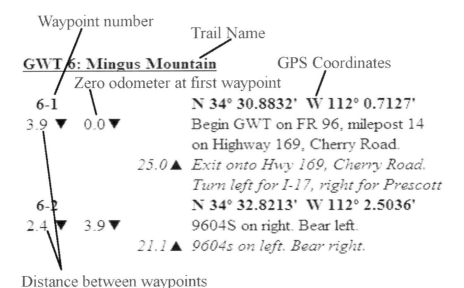

Waypoint number

Trail Name

GWT 6: Mingus Mountain   GPS Coordinates

Zero odometer at first waypoint

6-1   **N 34° 30.8832' W 112° 0.7127'**
3.9 ▼   0.0 ▼   Begin GWT on FR 96, milepost 14
                            on Highway 169, Cherry Road.
              25.0 ▲ *Exit onto Hwy 169, Cherry Road.*
                     Turn left for I-17, right for Prescott
6-2   **N 34° 32.8213' W 112° 2.5036'**
2.4 ▼   3.9 ▼   9604S on right. Bear left.
              21.1 ▲ *9604s on left. Bear right.*

Distance between waypoints

6-12   **N 34° 41.8904' W 112° 8.2890'**
1.4 ▼   23.6 ▼   Turn left to exit trail, turn right for
                            the Recreation Area
               1.4 ▲ *Turn right for Cherry. Recreation*
                     Area FR 104 straight ahead.
6-13   **N 34° 42.4342' W 112° 8.9399'**
Arrive 25.0 ▼   Exit onto Highway 89A. Turn left for
                            Prescott, right for Jerome.
              0.0 ▲ *Milepost 336. Mingus Recreation*
                    Area entrance.

Total mileage at waypoint   Zero odometer at first waypoint

Transferring Waypoint Coordinates to Your GPS Unit

It is easy to transfer the waypoint coordinates in this book to your GPS unit, but because of the vast number of makes and models (Garmin, TomTom, Magellan, Furuno), as well as the various computer operating systems (Windows, Apple, Linux), and the myriad software applications available for purchase or for free (Terrain Navigator, Fugawi, GPS TrackMaker), we cannot offer one explanation that will work for all.

The process of creating a route, however, is similar in all cases: either enter the map coordinates directly into your GPS unit, or enter them into a computer software application and then transfer the finished route to your GPS unit, either by a data cable that connects your computer to your GPS, or by copying the route to a memory card and then inserting it into your GPS.

If your GPS unit did not come with computer software, such as Garmin's MapSource or BaseCamp, you can find free software at www.maps-gps-info.com/fgpfw.html. EasyGPS is a popular program that works with many GPS units.

THE TRAILS

Great Western Trail 1:
Bulldog Canyon

This moderately difficult trail lies in the Goldfield Mountains south of the Salt River. It is in the state's Basin and Range Region with Butcher Jones and Needle Rock, Great Western Trails 2 and 3. Rainfall is minimal here, and tree-lined desert washes (streams) which are a prefect place to camp or picnic, can become roaring torrents in minutes after a heavy rainfall.

Although primitive, this trail is popular among campers, horseback and ATV riders, and is heavily traveled on weekends and holidays.

This trail travels through the Sonoran Desert and the Goldfield Mountains in the Tonto National Forest. The Usery and Goldfield mountains were the theater of the Arizona gold rush in the 1800s. In the nearby Superstition mountains, the Lost Dutchman Mine, more fiction than fact, was where Jacob Walz, a German allegedly found gold.

According to the stories, he would wander off into the mountains and eventually return with his donkey laden with the yellow ore. He existed, but any gold he brought back did not come from the Superstitions, since there is none there. Storytellers have added disappearances, gunshots in the dark, and mysterious footprints to the tale.

How to Get There:

To Waypoint 1: To arrive at the Blue Point Entrance Gate, drive north on Power Road from US 60 to Bush Highway/FR 204 and turn north. Drive approximately 13 miles on Bush Highway to the FR 10 Junction west of the Blue Point Recreation Site Bridge.

To Waypoint 4: (Difficult trail): From US 60, exit north at Idaho Road. Drive 4.5 miles to McKellips Road, then turn right. Turn left on Wolverine Pass Road, turn right onto Tonto Road and then left on Cactus Road to the gate at FR 10.

To Waypoint 5a: (Easy trail): From US 60, exit north on Ellsworth and drive north 8 miles to FR3554 and turn right. This entrance is 3/4 mile north of Usery Pass County Road.

You can get a detailed map of the area, a list of rules and regulations, and your OHV Access Permit at the Mesa Ranger Station.

Roads Comprising Trail: FR 10 and FR 3554. All routes other than these and 12, 1356, 3512 and 3556 are closed to motorized travel.

Open months/Best Travel: All year, but fall-winter-spring the best seasons because of the summer heat.

Permits: You will need a permit from the Mesa Ranger Station. This is not the same as the Tonto Pass. It is free and contains the padlock combinations to open the gates to the trails for a six-month period. The combinations are changed monthly.

Elevation Min/Max:
    FR 10 - difficult trail: 1451'/2230'
    FR 3554 - easy trail: 1451'/2215'

Paved Mileage: none

Unpaved Mileage:
    FR 10: 8.3 miles.
    FR 3554: 6.8 miles.

Travel Time:
    FR 10: 2.5 hours.
    FR 3554: 1 hour.

Difficulty: FR 10, difficult. FR 3554, easy.

Remoteness: 1/4. FR 3554 is well traveled to the point of congestion on weekends when campers and horse enthusiasts invade the area.

Services Available: None along trail. Full services are available at Apache Junction.

Driving the Trail: This is a primitive trail and you need a 4WD, high clearance vehicle with lockers on FR 10 at waypoint 3 (5.3 miles from Blue Point Entrance Gate). This is a steep descent down washed-out, rocky terrain before the trail curves sharply to the right and ends in a ravine. Driving skill and careful wheel placement are necessary.

Road Information and Contacts: Mesa Ranger Station, Usery Mountain Park Recreation Area (Appendix B).

Restrictions: This area is closed when there is a High Pollution

Advisory for particulate matter (PM10). Check with the Rangers or on-line before leaving home.

Trash dumping and other violations on this trail can result in fines of up to $5,000 and/or 6 months imprisonment.

Map References:

USGS Maps:

1:24,000: Apache Junction, Stewart Mountain.

1:100,000: Theodore Roosevelt Lake, Mesa.

1:250,000: Mesa (AZ)

Arizona Road & Recreation Atlas: p. 47, 81, 101.

USDA Forest Service Map: Tonto National Forest.

View from Trail

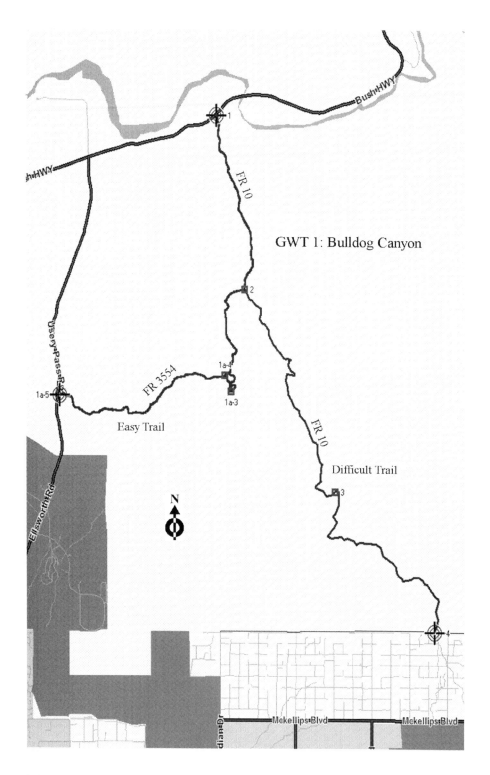

GWT 1: Bulldog Canyon

GWT 1: Bulldog Canyon Difficult Trail

1-1			**N 33° 33.0494' W 111° 34.8567'**
2.2 ▼	0.0 ▼		Enter FR 10 at Blue Point Entrance Gate.
		8.2 ▲	*Exit at Blue Point Entrance Gate.*
1-2	2.2 ▼		**N 33° 31.3354' W 111° 34.4682'**
3.2 ▼			Continue on FR 10.
		6.0 ▲	*FR 10 straight ahead.*
1-3			**N 33° 29.3315' W 111° 33.2216'**
2.8 ▼	5.3 ▼		Difficult descent into ravine.
		2.8 ▲	*Difficult ascent from ravine.*
1-4			**N 33° 27.9483' W 111° 31.8648'**
Arrive	8.2 ▼		Exit FR 10 at Wolverine Entrance Gate.
		0.0 ▲	*Enter FR 10 at Wolverine Entrance Gate.*

View of Trail   Trail Description

GWT 1: Bulldog Canyon Easy Trail

1-1			**N 33° 33.0494' W 111° 34.8567'**
2.2 ▼	0.0 ▼		Enter FR 10 at Blue Point Entrance Gate.
		6.7 ▲	*Exit at Blue Point Entrance Gate*
1-2			**N 33° 31.3354' W 111° 34.4682'**
1.6 ▼	2.2 ▼		Bear right into wash.
		4.5 ▲	*Turn left out of wash onto FR 10.*
1a-3			**N 33° 30.3277' W 111° 34.6503'**
0.2 ▼	3.8 ▼		Bear right.
		2.8 ▲	*Turn left.*
1a-4			**N 33° 30.4796' W 111° 34.7341'**
2.6 ▼	4.1 ▼		Washed out area.
		2.6 ▲	Washed out area.
1a-5			**N 33° 30.2809' W 111° 37.0079'**
Arrive	6.7 ▼		Exit trail at Usery Entrance Gate.
		0.0 ▲	*Enter FR 3554 at Usery Entrance Gate.*

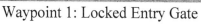

Waypoint 1: Locked Entry Gate   View of Trail

Great Western Trail 2:
Butcher Jones

This 27,000-acre recreation area is one hour from Phoenix and is open to all off-highway vehicles. It is named after "Butcher" Jones, in reality WW Jones, a doctor who grazed cattle in the area in the 1800s. Allegedly his nickname was ironic.

This trail winds though a sandy riverbed narrowed in spots by spiny brush. Your vehicle will be "Arizona Pinstriped" after you complete the trail. These are fine lines scratched onto your its finish by the overhanging brush and branches on the sometimes-narrow trail.

This is low desert and is home to rabbits, chipmunks, and quail that race ahead of your vehicle and slip off into the brush just before you think you will run over them.

How to Get There:
To Waypoint 1: From Highway 87, exit at Bush Highway (Exit 199), and drive east to the Butcher Jones Recreation Area. The entrance to the Rolls is in the rear but this will change in the future, so contact the Mesa Ranger Station before starting out.

Exit at Highway 87. Turn south for Phoenix, north for Payson.

To Waypoint 15: Enter FR 11 from northbound Highway 87. This is across from the Dos S Ranch exit off the southbound lanes. Use GPS coordinates for the exact location.

Exit at Butcher Jones Recreation Area.

Roads Comprising Trail: FR 1813 – FR 1343 – FR 401 – FR 1 43 – FR 11.

Open months/Best Travel: As in all the trails in the low desert, the spring, fall, and winter seasons are best. Flash floods are possible during the summer monsoons.

Permits: You will need a Tonto Pass to park or camp in a recreation area; you do not need a permit to drive or camp on the trail.

Elevation Min/Max: 1546'/2772'

Paved Mileage: None

Unpaved Mileage: 14.4 miles.

Travel Time: 2 hours 15 minutes.

Difficulty: Easy to Moderate. A high clearance, 4WD vehicle will have no trouble with this trail.

Remoteness: 1/4

Services Available: None along trail. The nearest services are at Fountain Hills and Mesa.

Driving the Trail: The southern portion of the trail is sandy and covered with numerous tracks that change after each flash flood. Therefore, the GPS coordinates may seem wrong at various points along the trail and the Rangers will warn you that you may get lost in the Rolls. Even so, you should have no trouble if you follow our map and GPS coordinates.

Drive in the widest tracks to keep pin-striping to a minimum. Also driving in tracks made by vehicles that have packed down the sand will help keep you from bogging down. You should air down before driving The Rolls.

Enter The Rolls (FR 1813) from the rear of the Butcher Jones Recreation Area. You can drive through it without a Tonto Pass, but you will need it if you decide to camp or picnic.

Continue in the sandy wash for about 5 miles until you cross FR 13 and enter FR 1343 (waypoint 4). You will cross two cattle guards before turning left on FR 401 (waypoint 7) in about 2 miles. Turn right on FR 143 at waypoint 8.

At waypoint 9 you begin a moderate descent down a steep, rocky, washed out road before leveling off again. This part of the trail is rocky and sandy until it exits onto Highway 87, but it is not difficult. Between waypoints 10-11 you will drive though Mesquite Wash; Rock Creek is between waypoints 12-13. Do not enter them if they are flooded. The "Stupid Motorist Law", (section 28-910 of the Arizona Revised Statutes), states that any motorist who becomes stranded after entering a flooded stretch of roadway may be charged for the cost of his rescue.

During flash floods raging waters can carry an automobile in a wash downstream. If you call public emergency services to rescue you, they may bill you up to a maximum of $2,000.

The north end of FR 11 is a popular area for target shooters. To my knowledge they prefer only paper or glass targets and are in an area east of the trail.

Road Information: Mesa Ranger District (Appendix B).

Restrictions: This trail is subject to closure when there is a High Pollution Advisory for particulate matter (PM10). Check before starting your trip.

Map References:

USGS:

1:24,000: Stewart Mountain, Mormon Flat Dam, Mine Mountain, Adams Mesa, Boulder Mountain.

1:100,000: Theodore Roosevelt Lake.

1:250,000: Mesa (AZ).

Terrain Navigator: Arizona South (AZ10)

Arizona Road & Recreation Atlas: p. 41, 47, 75.

USDA Forest Service Map: Tonto National Forest.

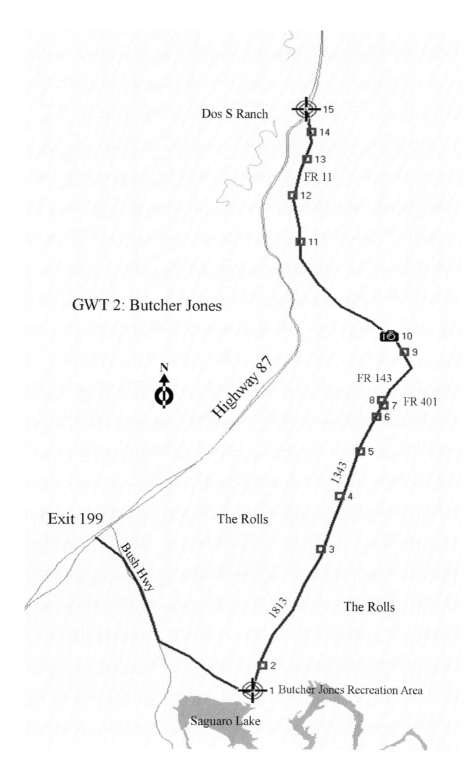

GWT 2: Butcher Jones

Dos S Ranch

15
14
13
FR 11
12
11

10
9

N

Highway 87

FR 143

8 7 FR 401
6

5

1343

4

Exit 199

The Rolls

Bush Hwy

3

1813

The Rolls

2

1 Butcher Jones Recreation Area

Saguaro Lake

GWT 2: Butcher Jones

2-1 — N 33° 34.6538' W 111° 30.8114'
0.6 ▼   0.0 ▼ — Enter FR 1813 from rear of recreation area.
14.0 ▲ *Exit Butcher Jones Recreation Area.*

2-2 — N 33° 35.1198' W 111° 30.6649'
2.9 ▼   0.6 ▼ — FR 1813 marker on right.
13.4 ▲ *FR 1813 marker on left.*

2-3 — N 33° 37.2557' W 111° 29.5215'
1.3 ▼   3.5 ▼ — FR 1813 marker on left.
10.5 ▲ *FR 1813 marker on right.*

2-4 — N 33° 38.2336' W 111° 29.1778'
1.0 ▼   4.8 ▼ — FR 13 on left. Go straight onto FR 1343.
9.2 ▲ *FR 13 on right. Go straight onto FR 1813.*

2-5 — N 33° 39.0565' W 111° 28.7913'
0.8 ▼   5.8 ▼ — Cattle guard.
8.2 ▲ *Cattle guard.*

2-6 — N 33° 39.6984' W 111° 28.4918'
0.3 ▼   6.6 ▼ — Cattle guard.
7.4 ▲ *Cattle guard.*

2-7 — N 33° 39.9005' W 111° 28.3549'
0.1 ▼   6.9 ▼ — Turn left onto gravel road FR 401.
7.1 ▲ *Turn right onto FR 1343.*

2-8 — N 33° 40.0047' W 111° 28.3931'
1.3 ▼   7.0 ▼ — Turn right onto FR 143.
7.0 ▲ *Turn left onto FR 401.*

2-9 — N 33° 40.8953' W 111° 27.9761'
0.5 ▼   8.3 ▼ — Begin moderate segment. Rocky,
steep and washed out road.
5.7 ▲ *End moderate segment.*

2-10 — N 33° 41.1832' W 111° 28.2542'
2.7 ▼   8.7 ▼ — End moderate segment.
5.3 ▲ *Begin moderate segment. Rocky,*
steep and washed out road.

2-11		**N 33° 42.8924' W 111° 29.9286'**
1.1 ▼	11.4▼	Bear right.
	2.6▲	*Bear left.*
2-12		**N 33° 43.7496' W 111° 30.0859'**
0.4 ▼	12.5▼	Straight onto FR 11.
	1.5▲	*Straight onto FR 11.*
2-13		**N 33° 44.4153' W 111° 29.8037'**
0.6 ▼	12.9▼	Bear left.
	1.1▲	*Bear right.*
2-14		**N 33° 44.9133' W 111° 29.7290'**
0.5 ▼	13.5▼	Stay on FR 11.
	0.5▲	*Bear right on FR 11.*
2-15		**N 33° 45.3289' W 111° 29.8258'**
Arrive	14.0▼	Exit to Highway 87.
	0.0▲	*Enter FR 11.*

Desert View   Dry Wash in the Rolls

Four Peaks   2-10: End Moderate Segment

It's not always as easy as it looks.

Great Western Trail 3:
Needle Rock

This is the last trail in the Basin and Range Region before you move on to the Central Highlands. It is also the easiest and the shortest, but since the off-road approach to Needle Rock is in a wash, the usual warnings about flash floods apply.

An oasis from the summer heat, you can reach Needle Rock either by paved road from Fountain Hills and Scottsdale, or by driving in Camp Creek, a wash that begins at Bartlett Dam Road. Interesting formations of mud and conglomerate rock line the wash.

At the Verde River there is a well-maintained campsite and the cone-shaped Needle Rock. You may see Bald eagles and Great Blue Herons in the area. A protected riparian area (Mesquite Bosque) on the other side of the river is off limits to hikers 6 months of the year.

Camping, picnicking, canoeing, fishing and wildlife observation make this a popular site. There are vaulted toilets and trash service, but no drinking water. Fishing and bathing are allowed, but require permits.

How to Get There:
    To Waypoint 1:
    From Cave Creek Road (FR 24) drive 2.9 miles east on Bartlett Dam Road (FR 19) and turn south onto Camp Creek (FR 413).
    To Waypoint 7:
    From Shea Boulevard in Fountain Hills, drive north on Fountain Hills Boulevard, turn right on E. McDowell Mountain Road and then turn north on N. Forest Road (FR 20). Drive through Rio Verde, Tonto Verde, and continue straight to the entrance to Needle Rock.
    From Pima Road in Scottsdale, turn east on Dynamite

Road and drive three miles to Rio Verde Drive. Continue on Rio Verde Drive to Forest Road (FR 20) and turn left. Needle Rock is three miles ahead. FR 20 is an unpaved road with narrow blind curves.

Roads Comprising Off-road Trail: Camp Creek Wash (FR 413)

Open months/Best Travel: Year round.

Permits: None to drive the trail. You can buy a Tonto Pass in many of the stores in the area if you intend to picnic or to camp by the river.

Elevation Min/Max: 1542'/2649'

Paved Mileage: 14.3 miles from Shea Boulevard in Fountain Hills to the Needle Rock campsite.

Unpaved Mileage: 13.3 miles from Bartlett Dam Road on FR 413.

Travel Time: 1 hour from Bartlett Dam Road.

Difficulty: Easy.

Remoteness: 1/4 from Fountain Hills, 2/4 from Bartlett Dam Road.

Services Available: None on the trail, but food and fuel are available at Rio Verde (three miles), Scottsdale, Cave Creek, Carefree, and Fountain Hills.

Driving the Trail: Camp Creek is a wide, sandy wash with numerous tracks that change after each flash flood, but all lead to Needle Rock. Since pin-striping is likely, follow the widest track where possible. It is a favorite trail among ATV enthusiasts, so be careful going around blind curves.

Road Information: Cave Creek Ranger Station (Appendix B).

Restrictions: The east side of Verde River (camping is on the west side) is closed to all entry from 1 December to 30 June.

Map References:
    USGS:
        1:24,000: Fort McDowell, Bartlett Dam, Wildcat Hill.
        1:100,000: Theodore Roosevelt Lake
        1:250,000: Mesa (AZ)
    Terrain Navigator: Arizona South, (AZ10)
    Arizona Road & Recreation Atlas: p. 41, 75.
    USDA Forest Service Map: Tonto National Forest.

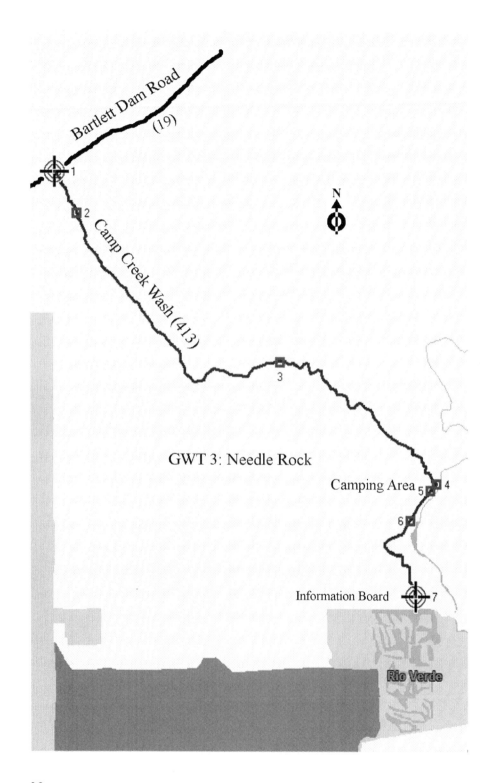

GWT 3: Needle Rock

GWT 3: Needle Rock

3-1			N 33° 50.9211' W 111° 47.1473'
0.9 ▼	0.0 ▼		Turn south onto Camp Creek (FR 413). from Bartlett Dam Road (FR 19).
		13.2 ▲	*Exit onto Bartlett Dam Road (FR 19).*
3-2			N 33° 50.3024' W 111° 46.7291'
5.5 ▼	0.9 ▼		Numerous tracks through sandy wash but all lead to Needle Rock.
		12.3 ▲	*Sandy wash.*
3-3			N 33° 48.1210' W 111° 42.8438'
4.2 ▼	6.4 ▼		Wash narrows between mud rock and conglomerate rock.
		6.8 ▲	*Wash narrows between mud rock and conglomerate rock.*
3-4			N 33° 46.3273' W 111° 39.8678'
0.1 ▼	10.6 ▼		Trail ends at camping area.
		2.6 ▲	*Camping area.*
3-5			N 33° 46.2359' W 111° 39.9806'
0.6 ▼	10.7 ▼		End dirt road.
		2.5 ▲	*Camping area. Begin dirt road to Needle Rock Recreation Area.*
3-6			N 33° 45.7917' W 111° 40.3732'
1.9 ▼	11.3 ▼		FR 2148 on right.
		1.9 ▲	*FR 2148 on left.*
3-7			N 33° 45.6820' W 111° 40.2688'
Arrive	13.2 ▼		Needle Rock information board.
		0.0 ▲	*Needle Rock information board.*

Scenery along the trail to Needle Rock

Great Western Trail 4:
Cave Creek to Bloody Basin Road and I-17

At 54 miles, this is one of the longest legs of the Great Western Trail. Cave Creek Road (FR 24) is open to Cadillacs and Bentleys until the Civilian Conservation Corps campground at Seven Springs, after which only 4-wheel drive, high clearance vehicles are recommended. The road may be impassable after a heavy rainy.

Cave Creek Road ends at Bloody Basin Road, which passes through the Agua Fria National Monument before it ends at Interstate 17. Many of the Indian ruins in the area have been incorporated into the Monument, which President Clinton designated in 1999.

The Information Board at the junction of Cave Creek and Bloody Basin Roads suggests the latter was named after its blood colored soils. Others say it refers to numerous Indian battles in the area. According to one historical report, after Apache Indians allegedly killed settlers, raided their livestock and stole their supplies, a posse tracked down and killed 100 of them, even though there was no proof they had committed the crimes.

This trail is in the Central Highlands Region of the state, a northwest-southeast band that separates the volcanic Basin and Range Region from the Colorado Plateau. Since this area receives the most rain of the three regions, you will leave sand and the Sonoran cactus behind and travel through pigmy forests of piñon and juniper trees, or larger forests of Douglas fir and Ponderosa pine.

You may see deer, javelina, mountain lions, bobcats and coyotes along this trail. Rockhounds will find agate at the junction of FR 24 and FR 269, and purple agate, jasper, and agate near Sheep Bridge.

How to Get There:
    To Waypoint 1: From Cave Creek, drive north on Cave

Creek Road (FR 24) to the information board 2.3 miles north of Bartlett Road.

To Waypoint 25: Leave I-17 at exit 259 and drive east on Bloody Basin Road (FR 269).

Roads Comprising the Trail: Cave Creek Road (FR 24) – Bloody Basin Road (FR 269).

Open months/Best Travel: Year round.

Permits: You need a permit to camp or to park in recreation areas in the Tonto National Forest. You can buy a day permit in stores in the area or online, but you will need to go to a ranger station to buy a yearly permit. You do not need one to drive the trail or to camp outside of the recreation areas.

You will also need a permit to drive on state lands. Contact information for the Tonto National Forest and Arizona State Parks permits is in Appendix B.

Elevation Min/Max: 2982'/4983'

Paved Mileage: 3.8 miles

Unpaved Mileage: 49.6 miles

Total Mileage: 53.4 miles

> Cave Creek Road to Bloody Basin Road:
> > Distance: 27.7 miles
> > Unpaved Mileage: 23.9 miles
> > Driving time: 1 hour 30 minutes
> Bloody Basin Road to Dugas turnoff (FR 667):
> > Distance: 14.1 miles
> > Unpaved Mileage: 14.1 miles
> > Driving time: 1 hour
> Dugas turnoff to I-17:
> > Distance: 11.6 miles
> > Unpaved Mileage: 11.6 miles
> > Driving time: 1 hour.

Total Travel Time: 3 hr. 30 minutes for the entire trail.

Difficulty: Easy to moderate.

Remoteness: 2/4

Services Available: None along the trail, but they are available at Cave Creek, Carefree and Cordes Junction.

Driving the Trail: Begin on Cave Creek Road at the information board 2.3 miles north of the Cave Creek Ranger station on Bartlett

Road (FR 19). The road is paved for several miles before changing to graded dirt and washboard gravel.

In about .3 miles you will arrive at the Sears Kay Ruin, the first "Point of Discovery" along the trail. This is a fortified Hohokam village from the 12th and 13th centuries that overlooks the Great Western Trail, Cave Creek, and Carefree. It is an easy hike to the ruins (but it is not wheelchair accessible) and worth a visit. The views are spectacular and interpretive signs at the site explain the village's features.

Seven Springs Wash at waypoint 6 and the CCC campground at waypoint 7 are recreation sites and a great place to picnic or spend the night. Several hiking trailheads are nearby.

From this point the trail gets rougher and a sign warns against driving it in a low clearance vehicle or in wet weather when the roads may be impassible.

At waypoint 12, where FR 24 ends, turn right for Sheep Bridge or left for Dugas (GWT 5) and I-17. The information board here describes the points of interest along the trail and gives a brief history of the area.

Sheep Bridge, which spans the Verde River, is at the end of a 12 miles long, rutted and rocky road. The drive will take about an hour. The bridge is not open to motor vehicle traffic and you will need to return on the same road. Its sandy beach is an ideal spot for fishing and picnicking, and a good place to camp.

The turnoff for Dugas (GWT 5) is at waypoint 16 (FR 677). This is a difficult, remote road; inexperienced drivers should avoid it. You cannot drive it in a low clearance vehicle.

After you pass the entrance to the privately owned Horseshoe Ranch at waypoint 21, the road dips to cross the Agua Fria River at waypoint 22. You can cross the river where it trickles over a concrete ford, but do not enter it if the water level is high.

Trail Information: Bradshaw Ranger District, Cave Creek Ranger District (Appendix B).

Restrictions: Seasonal. Check with Rangers or online for up-to-date information.

Map References:

Great Western Trail, Prescott National Forest Section.
USGS:

1:24,000: Humbolt Mountain, Cooks Mesa,

Rover Peak, Bloody Basin, Brooklyn Peak, Joe's Hill, Cordes Junction.

1:100,000: Bradshaw Mountains, Payson, Theodore Roosevelt lake.

1:250,000: Mesa (AZ), Holbrook (AZ), Prescott (AZ)

Terrain Navigator: Arizona South (AZ10)

Arizona Road & Recreation Atlas: p. 40-41, 74-75, 97.

USDA Forest Service Map: Tonto National Forest; Prescott National Forest.

Picnic Area in the CCC campground.

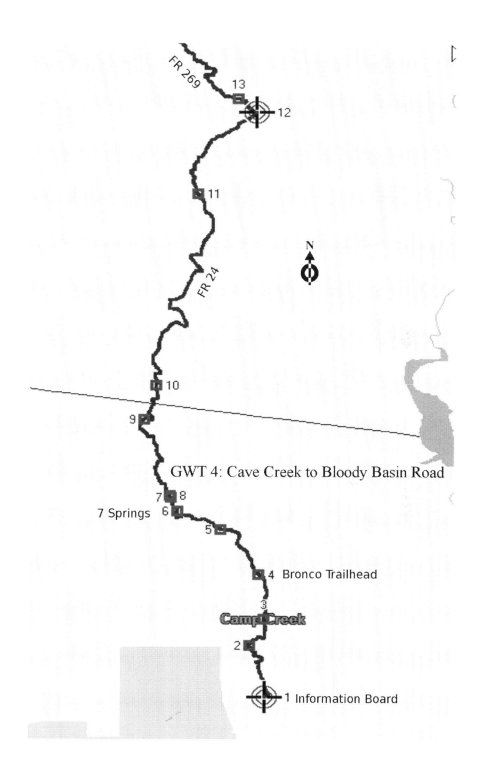

GWT 4: Cave Creek to Bloody Basin Road

FR 269

13

12

11

FR 24

N

10

9

7 Springs

7

8

6

5

4 Bronco Trailhead

3

Camp Creek

2

1 Information Board

45

GWT 4a: Cave Creek Road to Bloody Basin Road

4-1		**N 33° 52.6079' W 111° 48.9706'**
2.3 ▼	0.0 ▼	Start trail on Cave Creek Road
		2.3 mi north of Ranger Station.
	27.6 ▲	*End trail on Cave Creek Road*
4-2		**N 33° 54.0630' W 111° 49.4361'**
1.5 ▼	2.3 ▼	Pavement ends.
	25.3 ▲	*Pavement begins.*
4-3		**N 33° 54.8379' W 111° 49.0159'**
1.6 ▼	3.8 ▼	Wide, graded, washboard road.
	23.8 ▲	*Wide, graded, washboard road.*
4-4		**N 33° 56.1115' W 111° 49.1623'**
2.1 ▼	5.4 ▼	Bronco Trailhead. Permit required.
	22.2 ▲	*Bronco Trailhead. Permit required.*
4-5		**N 33° 57.3967' W 111° 50.3360'**
1.8 ▼	7.5 ▼	Campsite.
	20.1 ▲	*Campsite.*
4-6		**N 33° 57.9251' W 111° 51.6939'**
0.6 ▼	9.3 ▼	7 Springs Recreation area.
	18.3 ▲	*7 Springs Recreation area.*
4-7		**N 33° 58.2994' W 111° 51.8928'**
0.1 ▼	9.9 ▼	CCC campground.
	17.7 ▲	*CCC campground.*
4-8		**N 33° 58.3735' W 111° 51.9406'**
3.2 ▼	10.0 ▼	CCC trailhead 4. No services for 60
		miles. 4X4 recommended.
	17.6 ▲	*CCC trailhead 4*
4-9		**N 34° 0.5388' W 111° 52.7500'**
1.6 ▼	13.2 ▼	FR 41 on right. Bumpy but maintained.
	14.4 ▲	*FR 41 on left.*
4-10		**N 34° 1.5054' W 111° 52.3545'**
8.9 ▼	14.8 ▼	Campground.
	12.8 ▲	*Campground.*

4-11		**N 34° 6.9926' W 111° 51.0893'**
3.9 ▼	23.7 ▼	Wash in Round Tree Canyon.
	3.9 ▲	*Wash in Round Tree Canyon.*
4-12		**N 34° 9.3425' W 111° 49.2828'**
Arrive	27.6 ▼	Cave Creek Road ends.
	0.0 ▲	*Cave Creek Road begins.*

Authors' Jeep and off-road Teardrop trailer at the
junction of Cave Creek and Bloody Basin Roads

Signs along Cave Creek Road

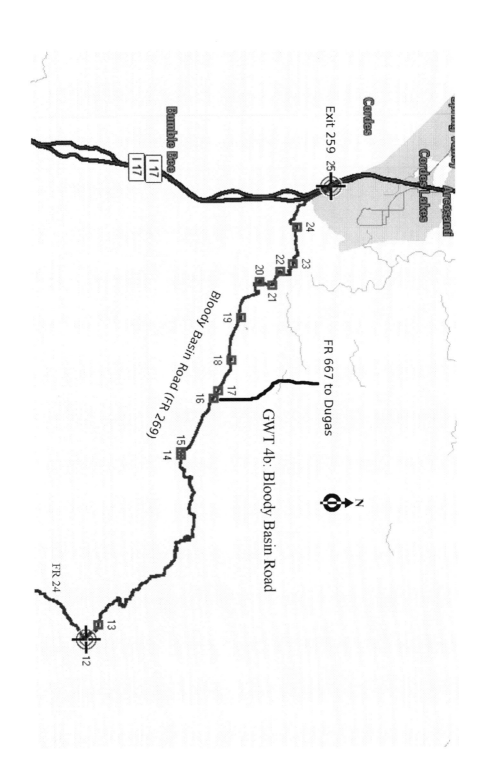

GWT 4b: Bloody Basin Road

GWT 4b: Bloody Basin Road

4-12			**N 34° 9.3425' W 111° 49.2828'**
0.8 ▼	0.0▼		Turn left on Bloody Basin Rd. to I-17 (or right for Sheep Bridge).
			Turn right on Cave Creek Rd. (or go straight for Sheep Bridge).
4-13		*26.1*▲	**N 34° 9.7220' W 111° 49.8392'**
10.6▼	0.8▼		Campground. FR 269 becomes 9269.
		25.3▲	*9269 becomes FR 269.*
4-14	11.4▼		**N 34° 12.3475' W 111° 56.5526'**
0.1 ▼			Cattle guard.
		14.7▲	*Cattle guard.*
4-15			**N 34° 12.3621' W 111° 56.6887'**
2.4 ▼	11.5▼		Cattle guard.
		14.6▲	*Cattle guard.*
4-16			**N 34° 13.3669' W 111° 58.7936'**
0.3 ▼	13.9▼		Turn off to Dugas on right.
		12.2▲	*Turn off to Dugas on left.*
4-17			**N 34° 13.5103' W 111° 59.1040'**
1.5 ▼	14.2▼		Cattle guard.
		11.9▲	*Cattle guard.*
4-18			**N 34° 13.9343' W 112° 0.3126'**
2.1 ▼	15.7▼		Bear left.
		10.4▲	*Bear right.*
4-19			**N 34° 14.2365' W 112° 1.9966'**
2.1 ▼	17.8▼		Bear left.
		8.3▲	*Bear right.*
4-20			**N 34° 14.8188' W 112° 3.4196'**
0.5 ▼	19.9▼		Rest area.
		6.2▲	*Rest area.*
4-21			**N 34° 15.2078' W 112° 3.2674'**
0.6 ▼	20.4▼		Horseshoe Ranch. Private property.
		5.7▲	*Horseshoe Ranch. Private property.*

4-22		**N 34° 15.4577' W 112° 3.7994'**
1.0 ▼	21.0 ▼	.Agua Fria River.
	5.1 ▲	*Agua Fria River.*
4-23		**N 34° 15.8548' W 112° 4.1253'**
1.5 ▼	22.0 ▼	Power lines.
	4.1 ▲	*Power lines.*
4-24		**N 34° 15.9908' W 112° 5.5507'**
2.6 ▼	23.5 ▼	Cattle guard.
	2.6 ▲	*Cattle guard.*
4-25		**N 34° 17.0677' W 112° 7.1698'**
Arrive	26.1 ▼	Exit to I-17.
	0.0 ▲	*Begin trail at Exit 259 on I-17.*

Bloody Basin Road   View from Bloody Basin Road

Sign and road in Agua Fria National Monument

Great Western Trail 5:
Bloody Basin to Dugas to I-17

Although most of this trail is easy, we rate it as difficult because of rock ledges and the climb out of Sycamore Creek onto a sandy bank, where you may need to air down and use lockers. In addition the section south of Dugas is remote and we recommend only experienced drivers in a high clearance 4WD vehicle attempt this trail in company with others.

Fred Dugas, the founder of the Dugas, was born in 1871 and came to the area with his father Louis in 1877. The family built their first homestead, "Indian Cabin," before building their second house farther south along Sycamore Creek. After the turn of the century Fred built his last house overlooking the creek.

The ranch had a blacksmith shop, a school, at two boarding houses and a post office, which opened in 1925. Many of the historic buildings are still standing, and the ranch remains in the family to this day.

The San Dominique Winery, located at the southeast corner of I-17 and State Highway 169 (Cherry Road – Exit 278), opened in 1978. In 1989 it started a "Fiesta Garlica," and now produces over 65 garlic-related items. You can find more information at its website: www.sandominiquewinery.com.

How to Get There:

To Waypoint 1: From Bloody Basin Road (FR 269), turn north on FR 677, which is 11.6 miles from I-17 or 14.1 miles from Cave Creek Road (FR 24).

To Waypoint 18: From I-17, take exit 278 and drive east on FR 732.

Roads Comprising Trail: FR 24 – FR 269 – FR 677 – 171 – FR 68D – FR 732.

Note that FR 732 is erroneously shown as FR 372 in the *Arizona Road & Recreation Atlas* and in the GWT section map, which is available for free from the Prescott Ranger districts.

Open months/Best Travel: year round, but the roads may be impassible during the rainy seasons.

Permits: You need a permit to camp or to park in recreational areas in the Tonto National Forest. You can buy a day permit in stores in the area or online, and must go to a ranger station to buy a yearly permit. You do not need one to drive the trail or to camp outside of the recreation areas, nor to drive the portion of the trail in the Prescott National Forest.

Elevation Min/Max: 3881'/5117'

Paved Mileage: 0 miles

Unpaved Mileage: 32.1 miles

Travel Time: 4 hours

Difficulty: Difficult

Remoteness: 4/4

Services Available: none along the trail. You can find fuel in Cave Creek or Carefree.

Driving the Trail: To begin the trail at waypoint 1, enter Bloody Basin Road at Exit 259 on I-17, drive east for 11.6 miles to FR 677 and turn north. The road at this point is rocky and rutted, but easy to follow in the grasslands. Bear left at waypoints 2 and 3. At waypoint 4 there is a Surveyor's marker from 1935.

You will pass through several gates on your way to Dugas. Remember to leave them (open or closed) as you find them. The road is not maintained and deteriorates as you approach waypoint 9.

Between waypoints 9 and 10 there is a short descent over rock ledges to Sycamore Creek. This is a difficult section of the trail and pin-striping is likely in its narrowest tracts. You will need a high clearance vehicle, 4WD, and possibly lockers to exit the riverbed onto the soft sand. If you have not already done so, air down your tires before beginning this section of the trail.

Turn left at waypoint 10 onto 171, Dugas Road. This road is maintained and takes you though the town where you will see many of its original buildings. Turn right at waypoint 12, FR 68D. There is a sign warning travelers not to enter this road when wet. If you ignore it, you risk a fine.

This is a primitive road but easy to drive as it passes through grazing land. Besides being home to horses, donkeys and cattle, it is where the deer and antelope play.

Turn left at waypoint 15. This appears as FR 372 on some maps, but on the Prescott National Forest Motor Vehicle Use Map and on the road itself, it is FR 732.

The road from here meanders in and out of a riverbed until it passes through an inhabited area and exits at I-17.

Trail Information: Bradshaw Ranger District, Cave Creek Ranger District (Appendix B).

Restrictions: None at this time. Check websites for further information.

Map References:
Great Western Trail, Prescott National Forest Section.
USGS:
1:24,000: Brooklyn Peak, Dugas, Arnold Mesa, Middle Verde.
1:100,000: Payson
1:250,000: Prescott (AZ), Holbrook (AZ), Mesa (AZ)
Terrain Navigator: Arizona North (AZ9)
Arizona Road & Recreation Atlas: p. 40, 74.
USDA Forest Service Map: Tonto National Forest; Prescott National Forest; Prescott National Forest Motor Vehicle Use Map.

Wpt 4: Surveyor's Marker

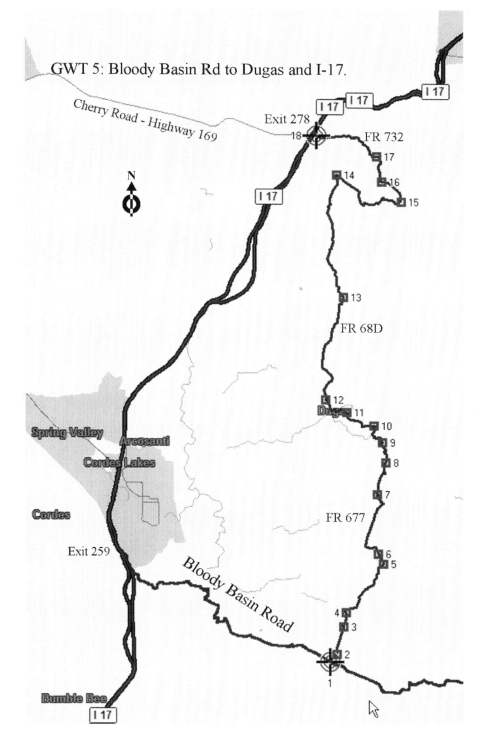

GWT 5: Bloody Basin Rd to Dugas and I-17.

GWT 5: Bloody Basin to Dugas to I-17

5-1		**N 34° 13.3637' W 111° 58.7924'**
0.4▼	0.0▼	Enter FR 677 for Dugas from Bloody Basin Road.
	31.9▲	*Trail ends at Bloody Basin Road. Right for I-17, left for Cave Creek.*
5-2		**N 34° 13.6078' W 111° 58.5447'**
1.1▼	0.4▼	Bear left.
	31.5▲	*Bear right.*
5-3		**N 34° 14.5124' W 111° 58.2527'**
0.6▼	1.5▼	Bear left at "y".
	30.4▲	*Bear right.*
5-4		**N 34° 14.9991' W 111° 58.1552'**
2.6▼	2.1▼	Surveyor's marker on left.
	29.8▲	*Surveyor's marker on right.*
5-5		**N 34° 16.6062' W 111° 56.6728'**
0.5▼	4.7▼	FR 605 on right. Stay on FR 677.
	27.2▲	*FR 605 on left. Stay on FR 677.*
5-6		**N 34° 16.9401' W 111° 56.8801'**
3.0▼	5.2▼	GWT on right.
	26.8▲	*Bear left.*
5-7		**N 34° 18.9355' W 111° 56.9055'**
1.4▼	8.2▼	9601D on left. Bear right on FR 677. Sign for Dugas 6 miles.
	23.8▲	*9601D on right. Bear left on FR 677 Sign for Dugas 6 miles.*
5-8		**N 34° 19.9941' W 111° 56.5678'**
0.9▼	9.5▼	Open & close gate on FR 677. FR 677A on right.
	22.4▲	*Open & close gate on FR 677. FR 677A on left.*
5-9		**N 34° 20.6610' W 111° 56.7237'**
0.5▼	10.4▼	Begin difficult descent to river.

		21.5▲	*End of difficult climb from river.*
5-10			**N 34° 21.2024' W 111° 57.0498'**
1.5▼	11.4▼		Turn left onto 171, Dugas Road.
		20.7▲	*Turn right onto FR 677.*
5-11			**N 34° 21.6458' W 111° 58.1625'**
1.1▼	13.0▼		FR 68F on left. Stay on Dugas Road.
		19.2▲	*FR 68F on right. Bear left.*
5-12			**N 34° 22.0833' W 111° 58.9609'**
4.5▼	14.1▼		Turn right onto 68D. Closed when wet.
		18.1▲	*Turn left on Dugas Road at stop. Wide, gravel, washboard.*
5-13			**N 34° 25.4795' W 111° 58.2702'**
5.2▼	18.5▼		Bear left.
		13.6▲	*Road on left. Stay right.*
5-14			**N 34° 29.5232' W 111° 58.5223'**
3.3▼	23.7▼		FR 9602A on left. Stay on 68D.
		8.4▲	*FR 9602A on right. Stay on 68D.*
5-15			**N 34° 28.6515' W 111° 55.9989'**
1.2▼	27.0▼		Turn left onto FR 732.
		5.1▲	*Turn right on FR 68D for Squaw Peak Road/Dugas Road.*
5-16			**N 34° 29.3176' W 111° 56.7544'**
1.1▼	28.2▼		Road follows and enters river bed numerous times.
		3.9▲	*Road follows and enters river bed numerous times.*
5-17			**N 34° 30.1519' W 111° 56.9554'**
2.8▼	29.3▼		Cattle guard.
		2.8▲	*Cattle guard.*
5-18			**N 34° 30.8321' W 111° 59.3348'**
Arrive	32.1▼		Exit at I-17. Follow directions for Flagstaff, Phoenix, or Prescott.
		0.0▲	*Exit I-17 at 278. Go east on primitive road FR 732 to Dugas.*

Narrow Passage

Friendly Inhabitant

Climbing out of the riverbed

Warning at beginning of trail

Old house in Dugas

Great Western Trail 6:
Mingus Mountain

The Mingus Mountain trail is a moderate bridge between two difficult trails, GWT 5, Dugas, and GWT 7, Smiley Rock. There is a campsite and recreation area at its entrance off US 89-Alt, after a warning the road is "not suited for wet weather travel or low clearance vehicles." Warnings similar to this appear in different versions on other legs of the Great Western Trail, and cars whose owners ignored them lie rusted and bullet-ridden in ravines along many of the off-road trails in the state.

How to Get There:
    To Waypoint 1: From I-17, exit 278, drive west on Highway 169 to milepost 14, and turn north onto FR 96.
    To Waypoint 13: From Jerome, drive south on Highway 89A to milepost 386 and turn left into the Mingus Recreation Area.
Roads Comprising Trail: FR 96 – FR 75 – FR 9004B – FR 132 – FR 413.
Open months/Best Travel: Spring-summer-fall. There may be snow on the mountain in the winter.
Permits: None.
Elevation Min/Max: 4465'/7551'
Paved Mileage: 2.3 miles
Unpaved Mileage: 22.7 miles
Travel Time: 2 hr. 30 minutes
Difficulty: moderate
Remoteness: 3/4
Services Available: none along trail. Food and lodging are available in Jerome, Clarkdale, and Cottonwood. Fuel is available only in Clarkdale and Cottonwood.
Driving the Trail: Aside from a few steep climbs and rutted roads, this trail should not be difficul for a high clearance SUV during

the dry summer season.

Starting at waypoint 1, FR 96 at milepost 14 on Highway 169, the narrow dirt trail runs through grasslands and is a popular camping area. Turn right onto 75, Hackberry Hill Road at waypoint 3. The road here is wide, gravel, and washboard until it is paved at waypoint 4.

Turn left at waypoint 6 onto Forest Mine Road, 9004B, where the pavement ends. At waypoint 7, bear left onto FR 132 at the Sutton sign in the wash.

Waypoint 8 is in an area still recovering from a recent fire. Turn left at waypoint 10 onto FR 413, and at waypoint 12, turn right to enter the Mingus Recreation area or turn left to exit the trail at waypoint 13. At the exit, turn left for Prescott, right for Jerome, or continue starlight ahead to begin Great Western Trail 7, Smiley Rock. This is a difficult trail and we will describe it in the next chapter.

Trail Information: Verde Ranger District (Appendix B)

Restrictions: None at this time. Check online or with the Verde Ranger Station before embarking.

Map References:

Great Western Trail, Prescott National Forest Section.

USGS:

1:24,000: Cherry, Cottonwood, Hickey Mountain.

1:100,000: Prescott.

1:250,000: Prescott (AZ)

Terrain Navigator: Arizona North (AZ9)

Arizona Road & Recreation Atlas: p. 40, 74.

USDA Forest Service Map: Prescott National Forest; Prescott National Forest Motor Vehicle Use Map.

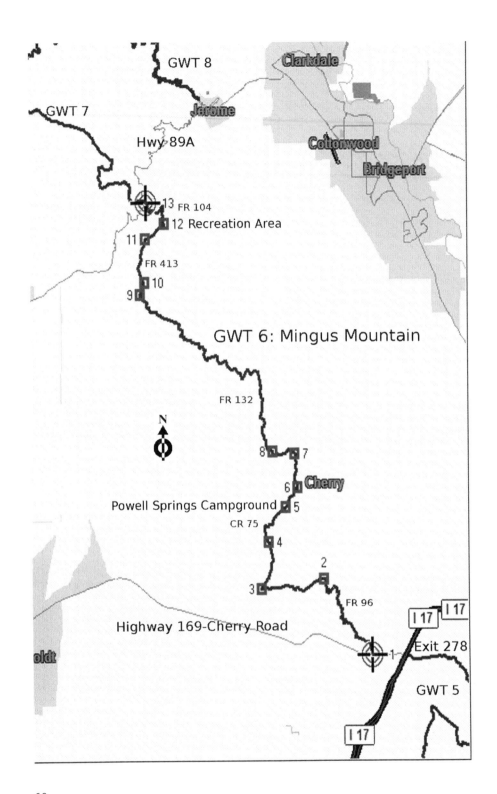

GWT 8

Clarkdale

GWT 7

Jerome

Hwy 89A

Cottonwood

Bridgeport

13 FR 104

12 Recreation Area

11

FR 413

10

9

GWT 6: Mingus Mountain

FR 132

N

8 7

6 Cherry

Powell Springs Campground 5

CR 75

4

2

3

FR 96

Highway 169-Cherry Road

I 17 I 17

oldt

Exit 278

1

GWT 5

I 17

GWT 6: Mingus Mountain

6-1
3.9 ▼   0.0 ▼

N 34° 30.8832' W 112° 0.7127'
Begin GWT on FR 96, milepost 14
on Highway 169, Cherry Road.

25.0 ▲ Exit onto Hwy 169, Cherry Road.
Turn left for I-17, right for Prescott.

6-2
2.4 ▼   3.9 ▼

N 34° 32.8213' W 112° 2.5036'
9604S on right. Bear left.

21.1 ▲ 9604s on left. Bear right.

6-3
1.5 ▼   6.3 ▼

N 34° 32.5741' W 112° 4.7803'
Turn right onto Hackberry Hill Road,
Road 75.

18.8 ▲ Turn left onto FR 96.

6-4
1.5 ▼   7.8 ▼

N 34° 33.7643' W 112° 4.5206'
Pavement begins.

17.2 ▲ Pavement ends, Hackberry Hill Road.

6-5
0.8 ▼   9.3 ▼

N 34° 34.6630' W 112° 3.8723'
Powell Springs Campground on left.
FR 372A.

15.7 ▲ Powell Springs Campground on right.
FR 372A.

6-6
1.1 ▼   10.1 ▼

N 34° 35.1492' W 112° 3.4298'
Turn left onto Forest Mine Road,
FR 9004B. Pavement ends.

15.0 ▲ Turn right at stop sign for Dewey.
Pavement begins.

6-7
0.9 ▼   11.2 ▼

N 34° 36.0327' W 112° 3.5349'
Bear left onto FR 132 at Sutton sign.

13.9 ▲ Sign for Sutton 9605E on left in
riverbed. Bear right onto 9004B.

6-8
8.9 ▼   12.1 ▼

N 34° 36.0675' W 112° 4.3581'
FR 9004A on left. Bear right.

12.9 ▲ FR 9004A on right Go straight.

6-9		N 34° 40.0889' W 112° 9.1733'
0.4 ▼	21.0 ▼	Straight on FR 132. FR 105 on left.
	4.0 ▲	*Straight on FR132. FR 105 on right.*
6-10		N 34° 40.3875' W 112° 9.0339'
1.4 ▼	21.4 ▼	Turn left onto FR 413.
	3.6 ▲	*Turn right onto 132.*
6-11		N 34° 41.5076' W 112° 8.9696'
0.8 ▼	22.8 ▼	Pack trail on left. Bear right.
	2.2 ▲	*Pack trail on right. Bear left.*
6-12		N 34° 41.8904' W 112° 8.2890'
1.4 ▼	23.6 ▼	Turn left to exit trail, turn right for the Recreation Area.
	1.4 ▲	*Turn right for Cherry. Recreation Area FR 104 straight ahead.*
6-13		N 34° 42.4342' W 112° 8.9399'
Arrive	25.0 ▼	Exit onto Highway 89A. Turn left for Prescott, right for Jerome.
	0.0 ▲	*Milepost 336. Mingus Recreation Area entrance.*

Sign and warning the entrance to Mingus Mountain

Great Western Trail 7:
Smiley Rock

Smiley Rock, or Martin Canyon, is difficult and remote. An experienced driver in a high clearance, 4WD vehicle with a spotter to guide him through the narrow, rocky spots will have little difficulty with this leg of the trail. If you have doubts about your ability or your vehicle's capability, bypass this leg and continue your trip north from Jerome on Great Western Trail 8, described in the next chapter. If you do decide to visit Smiley Rock, do not go alone.

Ample picnicking and camping sites are available on this trail, starting at Potato Patch Campground just off the highway at waypoint 1. The Woodchute Wilderness comprises most of the area enclosed by the trail, and is popular among hikers.

How to Get There:

To Waypoint 1: from Jerome drive 4 miles south on Highway 89A and turn north at milepost 336, across from GWT 6, Mingus Mountain.

To Waypoint 13: Drive 7.7 miles north from Jerome on Yavapai County Road 72, Great Western Trail 8.

Open months/Best Travel: year-round, but check weather conditions.

Roads Comprising Trail: FR 106 – FR 106D – FR 106E – FR 103 – FR 9701V – FR 318A

Permits: none at this time.

Elevation Min/Max: 5282'/7226'

Paved Mileage: 0

Unpaved Mileage: 15.1 miles for Martin Canyon plus another 8 miles to return to Jerome along the Jerome Perkinsville Road (GWT 8).

Travel Time: 2 hours 45 minutes for the drive through Martin

Canyon. One hour for the drive to Jerome.

Difficulty: Difficult.

Remoteness: 3/4

Services Available: None along the trail. Food and lodging are available in Jerome. You can get fuel and supplies in Clarkdale and Cottonwood.

Driving the Trail: Begin the trail at waypoint 1 at milepost 336 on Highway 89A. Once through the rest area, take FR 106 on the right. A parking area for the Woodchute Wilderness is at waypoint 3. Bear left onto FR 106D.

Bear right onto FR 106E at waypoint 5. The area straight ahead is closed to motor vehicles.

The most difficult portion of the trail, Martin Canyon, begins at waypoint 6 and ends at waypoint 11. In this section you will cross rocky washes and boulder fields in the canyon, and tight brush will pinstripe your car as you drive through it. Do not drive this trail if there is heavy rain forecast, since there is a real danger of flash floods.

Smiley Rock is on the north (right) side of the trail at waypoint 9.

At waypoint 11, turn right at the "T" and then left onto FR 9701V. Turn right on FR 318A under the power lines. This is a shelf road that winds around the north face of Woodchute Mountain.

The trail ends at waypoint 13. Turn right to go to Jerome or left to go to Perkinsville and Williams on the Jerome-Perkinsville Road (GWT 8).

Trail Information: Verde Ranger District (Appendix B).

Restrictions: none now. Check online and at the Ranger station for recent changes and weather conditions.

Map References:

Great Western Trail, Prescott National Forest Section.

USGS:

1:24,000: Hickey Mountain, Munds Draw.

1:100,000: Prescott

1:250,000; Prescott (AZ)

Terrain Navigator: Arizona North (AZ9)

Arizona Road & Recreation Atlas: p. 40, 68, 74.

USDA Forest Service Map: Prescott National Forest; Prescott National Forest Motor Vehicle Use Map.

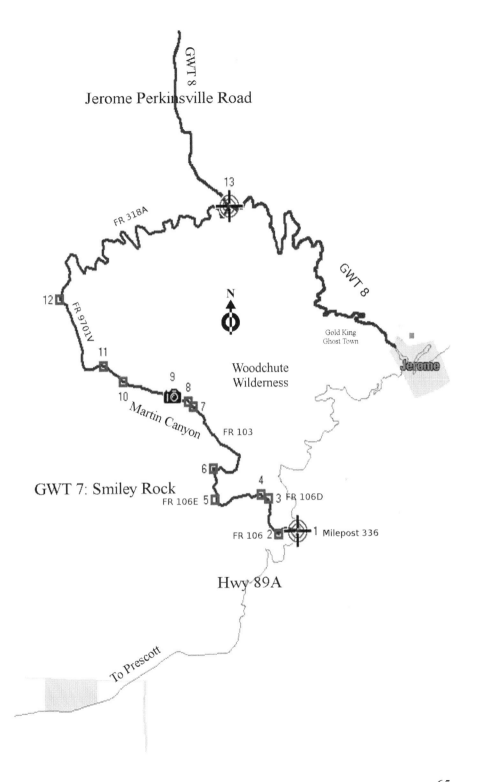

GWT 8

Jerome Perkinsville Road

13

FR 318A

GWT 8

Gold King
Ghost Town

N

Jerome

Woodchute
Wilderness

12

FR 970LV

11

9

8

10

7

Martin Canyon

FR 103

6

GWT 7: Smiley Rock

4

5

3 FR 106D

FR 106E

FR 106 2

1 Milepost 336

Hwy 89A

To Prescott

GWT 7: Smiley Rock

7-1   **N 34° 42.4399' W 112° 8.9658'**
0.4 ▼   0.0▼   Enter Smiley Rock Trail from milepost 336
                         on Hwy 89A.
        14.9▲ Exit trail onto Highway 89A. Turn right
        for Prescott, left for Jerome.

7-2   **N 34° 42.4027' W 112° 9.3658'**
0.7 ▼   0.4▼   Rest Area. FR 106 on right.
        14.5▲ Rest Area.

7-3   **N 34° 42.9174' W 112° 9.5725'**
0.2 ▼   1.0▼   FR 102 Woodchute Wilderness
                         on right. Bear left on FR 106D.
        13.8▲ FR 102 Woodchute Wilderness on
        left. Bear right onto FR 106.

7-4   **N 34° 42.9785' W 112° 9.7152'**
1.0 ▼   1.3▼   Gate.
        13.7▲ Gate.

7-5   **N 34° 42.9018' W 112° 10.6590'**
0.6 ▼   2.2▼   Bear right onto FR 106E. Area ahead
                         closed to motor vehicles.
        12.7▲ Bear left onto 106D.

7-6   **N 34° 43.3429' W 112° 10.6929'**
2.0 ▼   2.8▼   Turn right onto FR 103.
        12.2▲ Turn left onto FR 106.

7-7   **N 34° 44.2393' W 112° 11.1126'**
0.1 ▼   4.8▼   Go straight. FR 104 on right.
        10.1▲ Go straight. FR 104 on left.

7-8   **N 34° 44.3147' W 112° 11.2170'**
0.3 ▼   4.9▼   Sharp right turn.
        10.0▲ Sharp left turn.

7-9   **N 34° 44.3901' W 112° 11.5343'**
1.0 ▼   5.3▼   Smiley Rock on right.
        9.7▲ Smiley Rock on left.

7-10		**N 34° 44.6085' W 112° 12.5464'**
0.5 ▼	6.3 ▼	Tight brush. Stay on trail.
	8.7 ▲	*Tight brush. Stay on trail.*
7-11		**N 34° 44.8271' W 112° 12.9550'**
1.7 ▼	6.8 ▼	Turn right at "T" then left onto FR 9701V.
	8.2 ▲	*Turn left at "T" onto FR 103.*
7-12		**N 34° 45.7808' W 112° 13.8490'**
6.5 ▼	8.4 ▼	Turn right under power lines onto FR 318A.
	6.5 ▲	*Turn left under power lines onto FR 9701V.*
7-13		**N 34° 47.1049' W 112° 10.3399'**
Arrive	14.9 ▼	End of trail. Turn left for Perkinsville, right for Jerome.
	0.0 ▲	*Turn left on FR 318A.*

Along the trail

Waypoint 9: Smiley Rock

Great Western Trail 8:
Jerome to Williams

This 60-mile long trail is the longest leg of the Great Western Trail. It starts in the high desert of the Central Highlands and ends in the Colorado Plateau Region of the state, traversing forests of cedar, juniper, and piñon pine trees in the Prescott and Kaibab National Forests.

It is accessible to most vehicles, although travelers in low clearance vehicles would have to bypass FR 11 and FR 354 since these roads are unimproved and are not maintained for passenger cars. You should drive them in a 4WD, high clearance vehicle.

The Gold King mine and Ghost Town is just outside Jerome, and for a small fee you can see some of Arizona's mining history and assorted vintage automobiles. The Jerome State Historic Park with its magnificent Douglas Mansion is also worth a visit.

On the switchbacks north of Jerome is "First View," where you can get a panoramic view of the San Francisco Peaks in Flagstaff and the surrounding cites.

You can camp in the White Horse Recreation Area and fish for trout and channel catfish in its lake. Sycamore Point and the Overland Trail are also interesting stops along this trail.

How to Get There:
To Waypoint 1: Start at the Jerome Firehouse, Yavapai County Road 72.

To Waypoint 26: Turn south onto Garland Prairie Road, Exit 167 off I-40.

Roads Comprising Trail: From Jerome: Yavapai County Road (YCR) 72 – YCR 70 – FR 354 – FR 105 – FR 11 – FR 110 – FR 109 – FR 141 – Garland Prairie Road.

Open months/Best Travel: Year-round, but sections may be closed due to winter weather conditions.

Permits: None needed at this time.

Elevation Min/Max: 3818'/7005'

Paved Mileage: 1.3 miles

Unpaved Mileage: 58 miles

Travel Time: 4 hours.

Difficulty: moderate.

Remoteness: 1-3/4.

Services Available: none alone trail. Supplies are available in Williams, Jerome, Clarkdale and Cottonwood.

Driving the Trail: This trail begins at the Firehouse in Jerome and heads north on Yavapai County Road 72. This section is either paved or graded and is open to all vehicles, but it is tortuous and narrow in spots. Exercise caution when entering blind curves.

The entrance to Great Western Trail 7, Smiley Rock, is at waypoint 2. In about 8 miles you enter YCR 70. Follow this wide, maintained road to FR 354 (waypoint 6) and turn right. This is an unimproved road unsuited for low clearance vehicles.

At waypoint 8 you will pass the entrance to the Golden Buckskin Quarry, which is closed to visitors, before entering a rough section of mountain curves and grades. A ledge in the middle of the trail above the quarry requires careful wheel placement. If you have not already done so, air down and shift into 4-wheel drive.

The road becomes easier at waypoint 11, and at waypoint 13 turn right onto FR 105. Stay on this road until waypoint 17, where you turn left onto FR 11 and enter a heavily forested area.

At waypoint 19 turn right onto FR 110. This is the beginning of gravel roads open to all vehicles.

If you continue south on FR 110 you will arrive at Sycamore Point (you can also stay on FR 105 and then turn south on FR 110 instead of turning onto FR 11). This is a scenic area, and the canyon's red sandstone formations are well worth the detour. There is room to camp near the rim of the canyon.

At waypoint 20 turn left onto FR 109. The Overland Road Historic Trail crosses FR 109 at the Pomeroy Tank area. The U.S. Army built this road in 1863 during the Hassayampa Gold Rush to connect the goldfields near Prescott with Flagstaff Spring. Immigrants used this road until 1882, when the railroad across Northern Arizona replaced it.

At waypoint 23 turn left onto FR 141 and follow this to I-40 and the end of the trail. Along both sides of this road are the remnants of the railroad grade the Saginaw Lumber Company used in the 1800s.

Trail Information: Verde Ranger District, Williams Ranger District (Appendix B).

Restrictions: none at this time.

Map References:

Great Western Trail, Prescott National Forest Section.

USGS:

1:24,000: Clarkdale, Munds Draw, Perkinsville, May Tank Pocket, White Horse Lake, Davenport Hill, Sitgreaves Mountain.

1:100,000: Williams, Prescott.

1:250,000: Prescott (AZ), Williams (AZ)

Terrain Navigator: Arizona North (AZ9)

Arizona Road & Recreation Atlas: p. 34, 68.

USDA Forest Service Map: Prescott National Forest; Prescott National Forest Motor Vehicle Use Map; Kaibab National Forest Williams and Tusayan Ranger Districts; Great Western Trail Kaibab National Forest.

Thawing out the tent after a 20-degree night near White Horse Lake

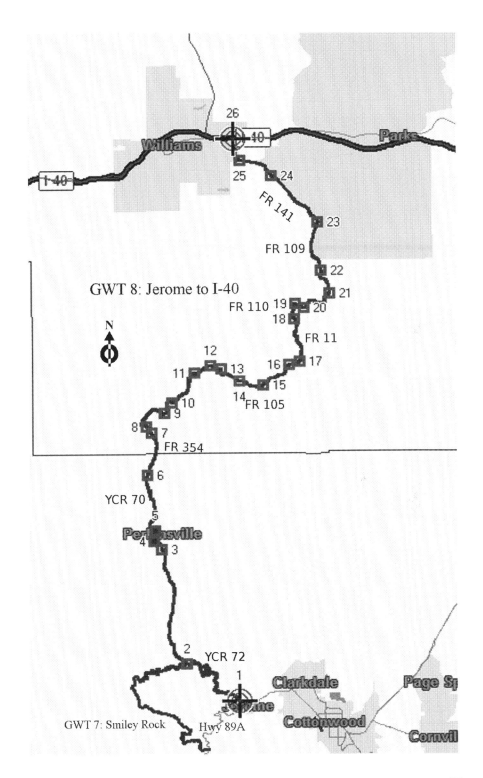

GWT 8: Jerome to I-40

N

GWT 7: Smiley Rock

GWT 8: Jerome to Williams

8-1   **N 34° 45.1106' W 112° 7.0150'**
7.7 ▼   0.0 ▼   Start at Jerome Fire House.
                           Yavapai County Road 72.
          59.2 ▲ End of trail. Turn right for Prescott
                 on 89A, left for Cottonwood.
8-2   **N 34° 47.1064' W 112° 10.3403'**
8.0 ▼   7.7 ▼   Smiley Rock Trail on left.
          51.5 ▲ Smiley Rock Trail on right.
8-3   **N 34° 53.2969' W 112° 11.8692'**
0.7 ▼   15.7 ▼   Perkinsville Road on left. Go straight .
                           on Yavapai County Road 70
          43.6 ▲ Perkinsville Road on right. Go
                 straight on Yavapai County Rd 72
8-4   **N 34° 53.7499' W 112° 12.3478'**
1.2 ▼   16.4 ▼   Turn left.
          42.8 ▲ Turn right. Perkins Ranch
                 straight ahead
8-5   **N 34° 54.2951' W 112° 12.2994'**
4.2 ▼   17.6 ▼   Road to Perkinsville on right.
                           Go straight.
          41.6 ▲ Road to Perkinsville on left.
                 Go straight.
8-6   **N 34° 57.3005' W 112° 12.7674'**
2.8 ▼   21.8 ▼   Bear right onto FR 354.
          37.4 ▲ Go straight on Yavapai County 70
8-7   **N 34° 59.5691' W 112° 12.5216'**
0.5 ▼   24.6 ▼   Bear left.
          34.6 ▲ Continue on main trail.
8-8   **N 34° 59.9305' W 112° 12.8203'**
2.5 ▼   25.1 ▼   Entrance to quarry on right. Begin
                           mountain curves and grades.
          34.1 ▲ Entrance to quarry on left. End of
                 mountain curves and grades.

8-9   N 35° 0.6152' W 112° 11.6830'
1.2 ▼   27.6▼   Entering Kaibab Forest.
          31.6▲ Entering Prescott Forest.
8-10   N 35° 1.2156' W 112° 11.2041'
2.7 ▼   28.8▼   Cattle guard.
          30.5▲ Cattle guard.
8-11   N 35° 2.7845' W 112° 9.8104'
1.2 ▼   31.4▼   End curves, mountain grades.
          27.8▲ Begin curves, mountain grades.
8-12   N 35° 3.2151' W 112° 8.7674'
0.7 ▼   32.6▼   Bear right. Stay on FR 354.
          26.7▲ Bear left. Stay on FR 354.
8-13   N 35° 3.0160' W 112° 8.1195'
1.6 ▼   33.3▼   Turn right on FR 105.
          25.9▲ End FR 105. Turn left on FR 354.
8-14   N 35° 2.3723' W 112° 6.9473'
1.6 ▼   34.9▼   FR 125 on right. Stay on FR 105.
          24.4▲ FR 125 on left. Stay on FR 105.
8-15   N 35° 2.1529' W 112° 5.4431'
2.2 ▼   36.4▼   Bear left on FR 105. FR 127 on right.
          22.8▲ Stay on FR 105.
8-16   N 35° 3.2346' W 112° 3.7983'
0.7 ▼   38.6▼   FR 138 on left. Stay on 105.
          20.6▲ FR 138 on right. Stay on 105.
8-17   N 35° 3.4150' W 112° 3.1507
3.1 ▼   39.3▼   Turn left on FR 11.
          19.9▲ Turn right on FR 105.
8-18   N 35° 5.7214' W 112° 3.4865'
1.0 ▼   42.4▼   FR 11H on left heavily forested area.
          16.8▲ FR 11H on right.
          Heavily forested area.
8-19   N 35° 6.5611' W 112° 3.4166'
0.6 ▼   43.4▼   Turn right onto FR 110.
          15.8▲ Turn left onto FR 11.

8-20		N 35° 6.2924' W 112° 2.8899'
2.3 ▼	44.0 ▼	Turn left onto FR 109.
	15.2 ▲	*Turn right onto FR 110.*
8-21		N 35° 7.0875' W 112° 1.2339'
1.7 ▼	46.3 ▼	White Horse Recreation Site on right.
	12.9 ▲	*White Horse Recreation Site on left.*
8-22		N 35° 8.3290' W 112° 1.7423'
3.3 ▼	48.0 ▼	Stay on FR 109.
	11.2 ▲	*Continue for White Horse Lake.*
8-23		N 35° 10.9430' W 112° 1.9393'
4.1 ▼	51.3 ▼	Turn left onto FR 141.
	7.9 ▲	*Turn right onto FR 109.*
8-24		N 35° 13.4552' W 112° 4.8837'
2.4 ▼	55.4 ▼	Continue on FR 141.
	3.8 ▲	*Turn left onto FR 141 at fork.*
8-25		N 35° 14.3032' W 112° 6.8961'
1.4 ▼	57.8 ▼	Right over RR crossing to Garland Prairie Road. Pavement begins.
	1.4 ▲	*Turn left on FR 141 after railroad crossing. Pavement ends.*
8-26		N 35° 15.4537' W 112° 7.2947'
Arrive	59.2 ▼	Trail ends at I-40. Go west for Williams, east for Flagstaff.
	0.0 ▲	*At exit 167 on I-40, turn south onto Garland Prairie Rd*

Views along the Trail

Great Western Trail 9: Williams to US 180

This trail travels through volcanic fields that surround Sitgreaves Mountain and Kendrick Peak, which are centers of silicic volcanism. Here you will see many rounded cinder cones (a small, cone-shaped volcano formed by the buildup of ash and cinders around a volcanic vent) as you travel over the Kaibab plateau.

Before you start this leg of the GWT, visit Williams, the "Gateway to the Grand Canyon." Apart from excellent food and lodging, it offers wild west entertainment, including the annual spring horseback ride to Phoenix by the Bill Williams Mountain Men, barbecues, arts and crafts shows, shootouts by the Outlaws from the Cataract Creek Gang, and the High Country Warbirds Air Display. Many events are scheduled during the various seasons, and you can get information about them at the Visitor Center at Second and Railroad, or online at www.williamschamber.com.

Laws Spring and the Beale Wagon Trail are the highlights of this trail. FR 2030 at waypoint 14 leads to a water hole and rock carvings from the 1858 Beale Expedition as well as Indian petroglyphs. Lt. Beale used camels to carry supplies to a crew of men forging a road to California through the wilderness. Thousands of travelers, from cattlemen to immigrants used this road until the Atlantic and Pacific Railroad arrived in the 1880s.

How to Get There:
To Waypoint 1: Exit 167, Circle Pines Road, on I-40, then drive north on Route 66.
To Waypoint 30: Turn south on FR 144 from Highway

180, 13 miles east of Valle, between mileposts 252 and 253.

Roads Comprising Trail: Historic Rte 66 – FR7 4 – FR 141 – FR 730 – FR 115 – FR 736 – FR 87 – FR 87E – FR 9161B – FR 9153H – FR 350 (354).

Open months/Best Travel: year-round unless snow or rain forces a temporary closure.

Permits: none at this time.

Elevation Min/Max: 6279'/7210'

Paved Mileage: 7.4 miles

Unpaved Mileage: 27 miles

Travel Time: 3 hours 15 minutes.

Difficulty: moderate

Remoteness: 3/4

Services Available: none along trail. Fuel, food and lodging are available at Valle and Flagstaff at the north end of the trail, and at Williams and Flagstaff at the south of the trail. You can also get fuel and some supplies at Parks, a small town on Historic Route 66.

Driving the Trail: This trail starts east of Williams, at Exit 167, Circle Pines Road, off I-40. The road is paved for 7.4 miles and then is intermittently improved gravel or improved dirt through its entire length. Parts of it may be impassable during the monsoon season.

To visit Parks, turn right at waypoint 4 and drive 6 miles on Route 66. To continue the GWT, turn left onto Coconino County 74 and stay on this graded road to waypoint 9, where you turn right onto FR 141. Turn left onto FR 730 at waypoint 10, and at waypoint 12, bear left onto FR 115.

The turn-off to Laws Spring and the Beale Wagon Trail, FR 2030, is at waypoint 14.

Stay on FR 115 to waypoint 17, where you turn right onto FR 736, which becomes FR 87 at waypoint 18. Continue on FR 87 until waypoint 26 where you turn right under the power lines onto FR 9161B (FR 350).

At waypoint 29 bear left onto FR 9153H. A GWT marker is on the right. Exit FR 350 to Highway 180. FR 350 is shown as FR 354 on the Information Board at the exit, however FR 354 is actually located in GWT 8, Jerome to Williams, between waypoints 6 and 13.

At Highway 180 turn left for Valle and Williams, turn right for Flagstaff, or go straight ahead to begin the Great Western Trail 10,

Tusayan to Indian Lands.

Trail Information: Williams Ranger District, Prescott National Forest (Appendix B).

Restrictions: none.

Map References:

USGS:

1:24,000: Sitgreaves Mountain, Squaw Mountain, Hubble Tank, Ebert Mt.

1:100,000: Cameron, Valle, Williams

1:250,000: Williams (AZ), Flagstaff (AZ)

Terrain Navigator: Arizona North (AZ9)

Arizona Road & Recreation Atlas: p. 34, 68.

USDA Forest Service Map: Kaibab National Forest Williams and Tusayan Ranger Districts, Great Western Trail Kaibab National Forest

Waypoint 9-30: Entrance to Trail from Highway 180

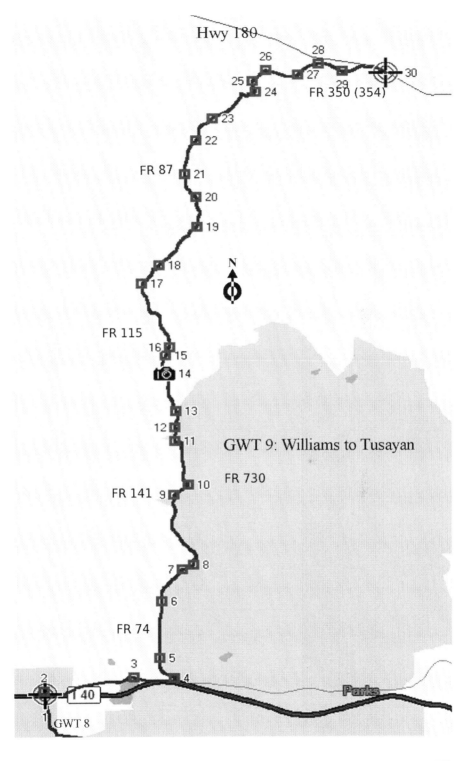

Hwy 180

28
26
25   27
24   FR 350 (354)
29   30
23
22
FR 87   21
20
19
N
18
17

FR 115
16   15
14

13
12
11   GWT 9: Williams to Tusayan
FR 730
10
FR 141   9

7   8
6
FR 74
5
3   4
2
I 40   Parks
1
GWT 8

GWT 9: Williams to Tusayan

9-1			N 35° 15.5304' W 112° 7.2965'
0.1 ▼	0.0 ▼		Begin trail from Circle Pines Road, exit 167 on I-40.
		34.5 ▲	*Circle Pines Road to I-40. Go west for Williams, east for Flagstaff.*
9-2			N 35° 15.6298' W 112° 7.3059'
3.0 ▼	0.1 ▼		Trail Location Map.
		34.4 ▲	*Trail Location Map.*
9-3			N 35° 16.0358' W 112° 4.3166'
1.4 ▼	3.1 ▼		Bear right.
		31.4 ▲	*Go straight onto old Route 66.*
9-4			N 35° 16.0172' W 112° 2.9616'
1.0 ▼	4.5 ▼		Turn left on Coconino County Road 74.
		30.0 ▲	*Turn right on Deer Farm Road.*
9-5			N 35° 16.6251' W 112° 3.4663'
2.0 ▼	5.4 ▼		Go straight.
		29.0 ▲	*Go straight.*
9-6			N 35° 18.3615' W 112° 3.3730'
1.3 ▼	7.4 ▼		End paved road.
		27.0 ▲	*Begin paved road.*
9-7			N 35° 19.3197' W 112° 2.6908'
0.4 ▼	8.8 ▼		Continue on FR 74.
		25.7 ▲	*Continue on FR 74.*
9-8			N 35° 19.4682' W 112° 2.3314'
2.8 ▼	9.2 ▼		FR 75 on right. Stay on FR 74.
		25.3 ▲	*FR 75 on left. Stay on FR 74.*
9-9			N 35° 21.5997' W 112° 2.9601'
0.6 ▼	12.0 ▼		Turn right onto FR 141.
		22.5 ▲	*Turn left for El Paso on FR 74.*
9-10			N 35° 21.9116' W 112° 2.4930'
1.8 ▼	12.6 ▼		Turn left onto FR 730.
		21.9 ▲	*Turn right on FR 141.*

9-11		N 35° 23.2449' W 112° 2.9409'
0.5 ▼	14.4▼	Stay on FR 730.
	20.1▲	*Junction FR 714 and FR 708 on right. Go straight.*
9-12		N 35° 23.6755' W 112° 2.9274'
0.6 ▼	14.9▼	Bear left onto FR 115.
	19.6▲	*Bear right onto FR 730.*
9-13		N 35° 24.1687' W 112° 2.8969'
1.4 ▼	15.4▼	707 on left. Go straight.
	19.0▲	*707 on right. Go straight.*
9-14		N 35° 25.3080' W 112° 3.2999'
0.7 ▼	16.8▼	2030 to Laws Spring, Beale Wagon Train Route on left. Stay on 115.
	17.6▲	*2030 to Laws Spring, Beale Wagon Train Route on right. Stay on 115.*
9-15		N 35° 25.8563' W 112° 3.2350'
0.3 ▼	17.5▼	FR 2029C on left. Stay on FR 115.
	17.0▲	*FR 2029C on right. Stay on FR 115.*
9-16		N 35° 26.1196' W 112° 3.1268'
2.6 ▼	17.8▼	Go straight. FR 779 on right.
	16.6▲	*Go straight. FR 779 on left.*
9-17		N 35° 28.0581' W 112° 4.0287'
1.0 ▼	20.4▼	Turn right onto FR 736 (FR 87).
	14.1▲	*Enter FR 115.*
9-18		N 35° 28.6358' W 112° 3.4386'
1.8 ▼	21.4▼	Bear left onto FR 87.
	13.1▲	*Go straight onto FR 736 (FR 87).*
9-19		N 35° 29.8017' W 112° 2.1930'
1.1 ▼	23.2▼	Bear left. FR 334 on right.
	11.3▲	*Bear right. FR 334 on left.*
9-20		N 35° 30.7015' W 112° 2.2268'
0.9 ▼	24.3▼	Cattle guard.
	10.2▲	*Cattle guard.*

9-21			N 35° 31.3996' W 112° 2.6004'
1.3 ▼	25.2 ▼		Corral on right. Go straight at intersection.
		9.2 ▲	*Corral on left. Go straight at intersection.*
9-22			**N 35° 32.4410' W 112° 2.2103'**
1.0 ▼	26.5 ▼		Stay on main trail.
		7.9 ▲	*Stay on main trail.*
9-23			**N 35° 33.0972' W 112° 1.6921'**
1.9 ▼	27.5 ▼		FR 313 on right. stay on FR 87.
		7.0 ▲	*FR 313 on left. stay on FR 87.*
9-24			**N 35° 33.9272' W 112° 0.2417'**
0.4 ▼	29.4 ▼		FR 330 on right. Turn left to stay on FR 87.
		5.1 ▲	*FR 330 on left. Turn right to stay on FR 87.*
9-25			**N 35° 34.2581' W 112° 0.3274'**
0.6 ▼	29.8 ▼		Bear right under power lines. FR 87E.
		4.7 ▲	*Bear left.*
9-26			**N 35° 34.5788' W 111° 59.9016'**
1.1 ▼	30.4 ▼		Turn right onto FR 9161B (FR 350).
		4.1 ▲	*Turn left under power lines onto FR 87E.*
9-27			**N 35° 34.4445' W 111° 58.8289'**
0.8 ▼	31.4 ▼		Turn left at fork.
		3.1 ▲	*Turn right at fork.*
9-28			**N 35° 34.7906' W 111° 58.1538'**
0.8 ▼	32.2 ▼		Bear right at fork onto FR 9161B.
		2.3 ▲	*Bear left at fork.*
9-29			**N 35° 34.5452' W 111° 57.3712'**
1.5 ▼	33.0 ▼		Bear left onto FR 9153H.
		1.5 ▲	*Bear right.*
9-30			**N 35° 34.5016' W 111° 55.9259'**
Arrive	34.5 ▼		End of trail. Exit onto Highway 180. Left for Williams, right for Flagstaff.
		0.0 ▲	*Start of trail at trail marker FR 354. (FR 350 on Trail Location Map)*

Waypoint 14: Road to Laws Spring

Views along the trail

Great Western Trail 10:
Tusayan to Indian Lands

This trail combines the high prairie and the pinyon and juniper forests of the Tusayan Ranger District of the Kaibab National Forest with the flat, almost barren Navajo Reservation. The former is well marked, with a turn-off for the Grand Canyon for those would like to visit one of the great wonders of the state before continuing the Great Western Trail. The latter is an adventure in itself since it will be easier to find a white buffalo in New York City than a trail marker on the reservation that will point the way back to civilization.

The Tusayan and Williams Ranger Districts are part of the largest contiguous pine forest in the world.

The Moqui Stage Station and route are part of this trail. This was the route of the stagecoach line that connected Flagstaff to the Grand Canyon from 1893 to 1901. The bumpy, dusty 20-hour ride cost a dollar a mile. Considering inflation, today's taxicabs cost less. The quality of the ride is open to discussion.

How to Get There:

To Waypoint 1: (Tusayan portion) From Route 180, 13 miles east of Valle between mileposts 252 and 253, turn north over a cattle guard and then onto FR 9161.

To Waypoint 37: (Navajo Reservation) turn south off Highway 64 between mileposts 276-277. Use GPS coordinates to locate exact entry point.

Roads Comprising Trail:

(Tusayan) FR 9161 – FR 305 – FR 305B – FR 301 – FR 313 – FR 312 – FR 337 – FR 2754.

(Navajo) 1345. Road markers are a rarity on the reservation.

Open months/Best Travel: Mid-May to November. This trail may be closed during the winter months because of snow or heavy rainfall.

Permits: None required to drive the Tusayan (southern) section of this trail. You need a permit to drive the northern section, which is on the Navajo Reservation.

Elevation Min/Max: 6342'/7103'

Paved Mileage: none.

Unpaved Mileage: 42.6 miles.

Travel Time: 5 hours 30 minutes.

Difficulty: moderate.

Remoteness: 4/4

Services Available: none along the trail. Food, lodging, and gasoline are available at Valle, at the junction of Highways 180 and 64, and in Cameron on Highway 89.

Driving the Trail:

The trail starts on Highway 180, 13 miles east of Valle between mileposts 252 and 253. The trail is unmarked here, but it begins directly across from the end of GWT 9. Turn north over a wide cattle guard and then left onto FR 9161.

The rutted trail has rocky, bumpy sections, but it is easy to easy drive. Secondary trails bypass any muddy sections that might be present after heavy rains.

It begins in the high desert of the Kaibab Forest where only grasses and scattered trees mark the landscape. After a few miles you leave the forest and enter Babbitt's Coconino Plateau Natural Reserve Lands, but will reenter the forest when FR 9161 becomes FR 305, just before waypoint 6.

At waypoint 7 you arrive at the Moqui Stage Station information board. The remains of the stage stop are just past FR 301 in the Russell Wash Section of the Arizona Trail.

You can continue on FR 305 to FR 320 and Route 64 to visit the Grand Canyon, or turn right onto FR 305B to stay on the GWT.

You will pass the Harbison and Bloody Tanks (both reservoirs) near waypoint 10 before turning left on FR 313 at waypoint 12. At waypoint 16, turn right onto FR 312. Stay on this road to FR 337 at waypoint 19. Enter FR 2754 at waypoint 20. There is an active sinkhole near here.

The information board at waypoint 21 signals the end of the Tusayan portion of the trail.

As the Navajo Reservation is not part of the GWT, you can return to Highway 180, or you can drive across the reservation and exit the trail at Highway 64.

The road markings on the reservation are scarce to nonexistent. There are many roads in this area, some of which have not been traveled in a very long time. Follow our trail or make your own. An Arizona Topographical map, compatible with Garmin GPS receivers, shows many of the trails crossing the reservation. You can download it for free at www.gpsfiledepot.com/maps/view/1.

If you drive through the reservation, there is a spectacular view of the Little Colorado River Gorge at waypoint 33.

This trail ends at Highway 64, but rather than drive immediately to House Rock and Great Western Trail 11, stop at the Navajo Ranger Station (at the junction of Highways 89 and 64) in Cameron and buy a permit to visit and camp on the reservation at The Gap.

Trail Information: Tusayan Ranger District, Navajo Ranger Station (Appendix B).

Restrictions: You need a permit to drive or camp on the Navajo Reservation.

Map References:
USGS:
1:24,000: Ebert Mt, Dog Knobs, Harbison Tank, Peterson Flat, Willows Camp, Hellhole Bend.
1:100,000: Cameron.
1:250,000: Flagstaff (AZ)
Terrain Navigator: Arizona North (AZ9)
Arizona Road & Recreation Atlas: p. 34, 68.
USDA Forest Service Map: Kaibab National Forest Williams and Tusayan Ranger Districts, Great Western Trail Kaibab National Forest.

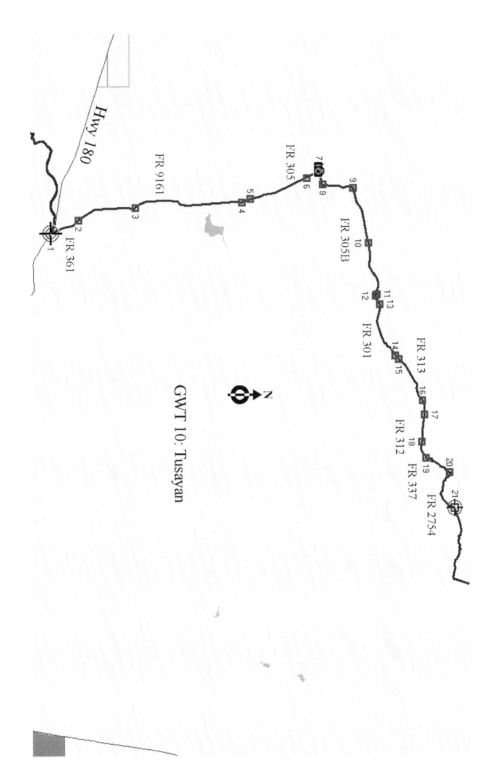

GWT 10: Tusayan

GWT 10: Tusayan to Navajo Reservation

10-1   N 35° 34.5211' W 111° 55.9214'
1.4 ▼ 0.0▼   Turn north from US 180 between mile markers 252-253, then left onto FR 9161.

       42.4 ▲ *Exit onto US 180. Turn right for Williams, left for Flagstaff.*

10-2   N 35° 35.6500' W 111° 56.5296'
2.7 ▼ 1.4▼   Bear left at fork. Washed out areas.

       41.0 ▲ *Go straight.*

10-3   N 35° 37.9245' W 111° 57.1262'
5.1 ▼ 4.1▼   Bear left.

       38.3 ▲ *Go straight.*

10-4   N 35° 42.1839' W 111° 57.3522'
0.4 ▼ 9.2▼   Bear left.

       33.2 ▲ *Bear right.*

10-5   N 35° 42.5351' W 111° 57.5130'
2.7 ▼ 9.6▼   Bear right.

       32.8 ▲ *Go straight.*

10-6   N 35° 44.7776' W 111° 58.5388'
0.7 ▼ 12.3▼   Bear left at "y." FR 2737 on right.

       30.1 ▲ *Go straight.*

10-7   N 35° 45.2951' W 111° 58.9253'
0.7 ▼ 13.0▼   Moqui Stage Station information board. Turn right on FR 305B.

       29.4 ▲ *Turn left onto FR 305.*

10-8   N 35° 45.4116' W 111° 58.2274'
1.5 ▼ 13.7▼   FR 2737 on right. Go straight.

       28.7 ▲ *Bear right. FR 2737 on left.*

10-9   N 35° 46.6208' W 111° 58.0465'
2.6 ▼ 15.2▼   Turn right onto FR 305B.

       27.2 ▲ *Bear left on FR 305B.*

10-10   N 35° 47.2207' W 111° 55.4108'
2.5 ▼ 17.8▼   FR 305BA on left. Go straight.

       24.6 ▲ *FR 305BA on right. Bear left.*

10-11		N 35° 47.5613' W 111° 52.9162'
0.1 ▼	20.3 ▼	Junction FR 301. Turn right on FR 301
	22.2 ▲	*Turn left on FR 305B.*
10-12		N 35° 47.5070' W 111° 52.8632'
0.5 ▼	20.4 ▼	FR 301 straight ahead. Turn left on FR 313.
	22.1 ▲	*Turn right on FR 301.*
10-13		N 35° 47.6891' W 111° 52.4437'
2.6 ▼	20.9 ▼	Russel Wash Section. AZ Trail on left.
	21.6 ▲	*Russel Wash Section. AZ Trail on right.*
10-14		N 35° 48.2852' W 111° 49.9883'
0.2 ▼	23.5 ▼	FR 313 F on left. Go straight.
	19.0 ▲	*FR 313 F on right. Go straight.*
10-15		N 35° 48.4302' W 111° 49.7962'
2.2 ▼	23.7 ▼	Cross FR 2741. Go straight on FR 313.
	18.8 ▲	*Cross FR 2741. Go straight on FR 313.*
10-16		N 35° 49.3638' W 111° 47.8190'
0.7 ▼	25.9 ▼	FR 313 on left. Go right on FR 312.
	16.6 ▲	*Go straight on FR 313.*
10-17		N 35° 49.4693' W 111° 47.1417'
1.3 ▼	26.6 ▼	Bear right. Stay on FR 312.
	15.9 ▲	*Bear left on FR 312.*
10-18		N 35° 49.3387' W 111° 45.8105'
0.8 ▼	27.9 ▼	FR 2763 on right. Go straight.
	14.6 ▲	*FR 2763 on left. Go straight.*
10-19		N 35° 49.5245' W 111° 45.0413'
1.4 ▼	28.7 ▼	FR 312 on right. Go straight on FR 337.
	13.8 ▲	*Bear right onto FR 312.*
10-20		N 35° 50.4640' W 111° 44.3510'
2.2 ▼	30.1 ▼	Go right on FR 2754.
	12.4 ▲	*Go straight.*
10-21		N 35° 50.6646' W 111° 42.6272'
0.1 ▼	32.3 ▼	End of GWT. Bear right after cattle guard.
	10.2 ▲	*Follow road to left*

Views along the Trail

Waypoint 7: Moqui Stage Station Information Board

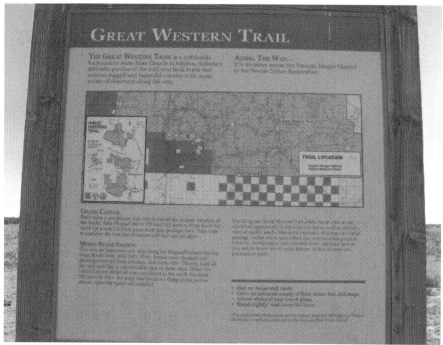

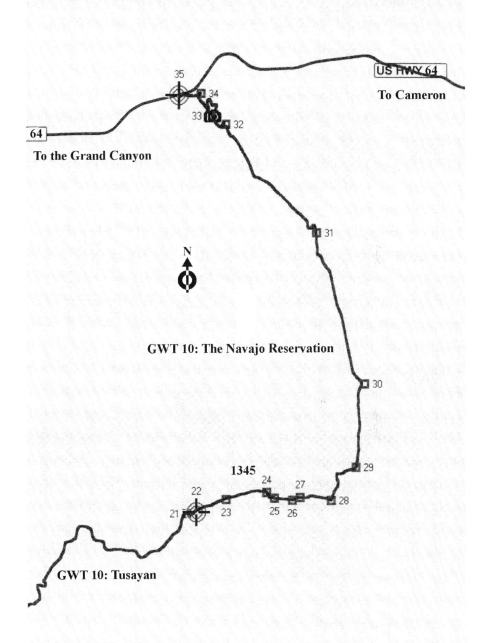

US HWY 64

To Cameron

35

34

33

32

64

To the Grand Canyon

31

N

GWT 10: The Navajo Reservation

30

29

1345

24

27

22

28

21

23

25 26

GWT 10: Tusayan

GWT 10: Navajo Reservation to Highway 64

10-22   N 35° 50.6907'   W 111° 42.4736'
  0.5 ▼   32.4 ▼   Go straight.
                    10.1 ▲ *Go straight.*
10-23   N 35° 50.8429'   W 111° 41.9999'
  0.6 ▼   32.9 ▼   Go straight.
                    9.6 ▲ *Go straight.*
10-24   N 35° 50.9280'   W 111° 41.3535'
  0.2 ▼   33.5 ▼   Bear right.
                    9.0 ▲ *Bear left onto 1345.*
10-25   N 35° 50.8501'   W 111° 41.2129'
  0.3 ▼   33.7 ▼   Go straight.
                    8.8 ▲ *Go straight.*
10-26   N 35° 50.8337'   W 111° 40.9464'
  0.1 ▼   34.0 ▼   Bear left.
                    8.5 ▲ *Go straight.*
10-27   N 35° 50.8679'   W 111° 40.8238'
  0.5 ▼   34.1 ▼   Bear right.
                    8.4 ▲ *Bear left.*
10-28   N 35° 50.8314'   W 111° 40.3387'
  0.7 ▼   34.6 ▼   Bear left.
                    7.9 ▲ *Bear right.*
10-29   N 35° 51.2581'   W 111° 39.9309'
  1.2 ▼   35.3 ▼   Bear left then go straight.
                    7.2 ▲ *Bear right.*
10-30   N 35° 52.2833'   W 111° 39.8517'
  2.3 ▼   36.5 ▼   Turn left.
                    6.0 ▲ *Bear right.*
10-31   N 35° 54.1659'   W 111° 40.5782'
  2.2 ▼   38.8 ▼   Trail on right. Go straight.
                    3.7 ▲ *Trail on left. Go straight.*
10-32   N 35° 55.5040'   W 111° 42.0651'
  0.3 ▼   41.0 ▼   Camping area on right.
                    1.5 ▲ *Camping area on left.*

10-33		N 35° 55.6128' W 111° 42.2325'
0.8 ▼	41.3 ▼	Trail on left. Bear right.
	1.2 ▲	*Bear left then go straight.*
10-34		N 35° 55.8955' W 111° 42.4151'
0.4 ▼	42.2 ▼	Turn left.
	0.4 ▲	*Turn right.*
10-35		N 35° 55.8708' W 111° 42.7643'
Arrive	42.5 ▼	End of trail at Hwy 64. Turn left for Grand Canyon, right for Cameron.
	0.0 ▲	*Begin trail, turn south between mile markers 276-277.*

Modern cattle roundup on the reservation.

Old hogan on the reservation.

Waypoint 33: Little Colorado River Gorge.

94

Great Western Trail 11:
House Rock to Jacob Lake (US 89A)

The scenery along Highway 89 from GWT 10 to GWT 11 through the Painted Desert is spectacular. A clay called bentonite that swells when wet and erodes away when dry, makes up the Chinle Formation. Few plants can grow here, but lavender, blue, green, and gray hills make up for what the area lacks in vegetation,.

Highway 89 continues to Page, but you will turn onto 89-Alt and drive over the Navajo Bridge that crosses the Colorado River in Marble Canyon. The highway runs along the south side of the Vermilion Cliffs. Navajo Sandstone, a pale, salmon-colored formation with slanting layers, is prominent in this area.

This trail begins at House Rock and its bison herd, with a difficult ascent after a confusing drive though miles of unmarked grasslands. Much of it traverses forested lands, some of which burned in a recent fire. Many of the trees killed then are now falling across the trail, creating an obstacle course that changes from day to day. If you cannot drive around them, you will have to saw or hack through them.

This is a difficult, remote trail, and a sign at the beginning of a long, steep, and slippery ascent warns you not to try the climb in a 2WD vehicle.

How to Get There:
    To Waypoint 1: Turn south on FR 8910, House Rock, between mileposts 559 and 560 on US 89A.
    To Waypoint 27: Turn south on FR 225 at milepost 576 on US 89A (near Jacob Lake).
    Roads Comprising Trail: (From House Rock) FR 8910 – FR 284C – FR 284 – FR 224 – FR 225.
    Open months/Best Travel: Mid-May to November. It may be closed because of snow and rain between December and May.

Permits: none at this time.

Elevation Min/Max: 4924'/8528'

Mileage: 27. 6 miles.

Unpaved Mileage: 27.6 miles.

Time: 3 hours.

Difficulty: Difficult

Remoteness: 4/4

Services: none. Fuel, food and lodging are available at Marble Canyon and Jacob Lake.

Driving the Trail: The trail begins on a graded road at House Rock, FR 8910, between mileposts 559 and 560. The information board at the entrance to the trail explains the history of the area.

At waypoint 2, turn right 50 yards before the cattle guard sign into a pasture, or continue on to a small, primitive campground to spend the night.

There may be no tracks through the grassland from waypoint 2 to waypoint 7, so follow the GPS coordinates carefully.

At waypoint 5, go around a watering hole and bear left. At waypoint 9 there is a warning not to continue if you are not driving a 4WD vehicle. A long ascent begins here, needing careful wheel placement, and ends at waypoint 11.

Enter FR 284C at waypoint 12. Stay on this road, which is rocky and off-camber in spots, until you pass a water tank on the left. Follow the road downhill and bear left. At waypoint 14 turn right over the cattle guard and then turn left. This road it is FR 224, even though it and the one you just left are both FR 284. Continue on FR 224 and cross FR 220 at waypoint 15.

At waypoint 16 the trail climbs for the next 5.5 miles. Many burned trees have fallen across the road in this area, and you will have to find your way around them. Wildlife abounds, and you will see deer and other animals scamper through the burned-out forest.

The road levels out at waypoint 20. At waypoint 21 turn right onto FR 225. Stay on this road until you exit the trail at US 89A, south of Jacob Lake. There are many areas to camp along this trail, which apart from FR 225, is remote.

Trail Information: North Kaibab Ranger District (Appendix B).

Restrictions: none at this time.

Map References:

USGS:
1:24,000: Emmett Hill, House Rock, Jacob Lake.

1:100,000: Fredonia, Glen Canyon dam.
1:250,000: Marble Canyon, Grand Canyon
Terrain Navigator: Arizona North (AZ9)
Arizona Road & Recreation Atlas: p. 28, 62.
USDA Forest Service Map: Kaibab National Forest North Kaibab Ranger District; Great Western Trail Kaibab National Forest.

Marble Canyon

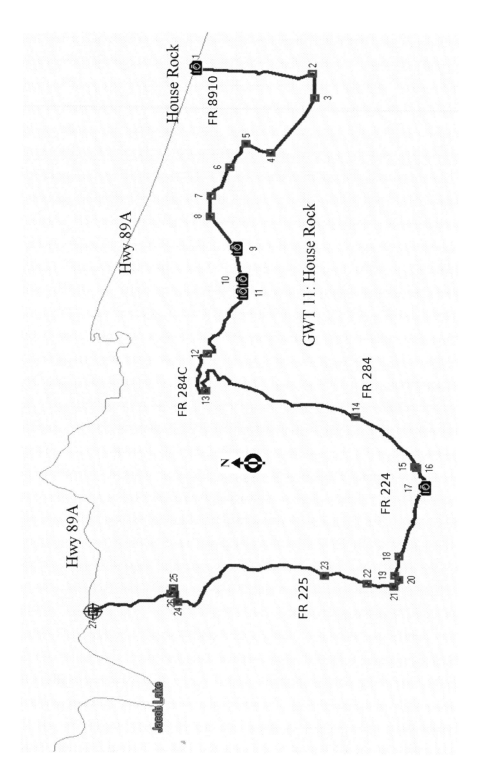

GWT 11: House Rock

House Rock

FR 8910

FR 284C

FR 284

FR 224

FR 225

Hwy 89A

Great Lake

N

GWT 11: House Rock to Highway 89A

11-1		**N 36° 42.2896' W 111° 56.7648'**
2.3 ▼	0.0 ▼	Turn south onto FR 8910, House Rock between mileposts 559 and 560.
	27.5 ▲	*Exit at US 89A. Turn left for Jacob Lake, right for Marble Canyon.*
11-2		**N 36° 40.3499' W 111° 56.9068'**
0.6 ▼	2.3 ▼	Turn right here, 50 yards before cattle guard sign.
	25.2 ▲	*Turn left on wide road.*
11-3		**N 36° 40.3074' W 111° 57.5205'**
1.5 ▼	2.9 ▼	Bear right.
	24.6 ▲	*Turn left.*
11-4		**N 36° 41.0273' W 111° 58.9113'**
0.5 ▼	4.4 ▼	Turn right.
	23.1 ▲	*Turn left.*
11-5		**N 36° 41.4466' W 111° 58.6724'**
0.6 ▼	4.9 ▼	Turn left.
	22.6 ▲	*Turn right.*
11-6		**N 36° 41.7149' W 112° 59.2654'**
0.8 ▼	5.5 ▼	Go around watering hole. Bear left.
	22.0 ▲	*Go around watering hole. Bear left.*
11-7		**N 36° 42.0260' W 112° 59.9964'**
0.5 ▼	6.3 ▼	Bear left.
	21.2 ▲	*Bear right.*
11-8		**N 36° 42.0280' W 112° 0.5158'**
0.9 ▼	6.8 ▼	Bear left.
	20.7 ▲	*Bear right.*
11-9		**N 36° 41.5979' W 112° 1.3272'**
0.8 ▼	7.7 ▼	Four Wheel Drive sign. Begin ascent.
	19.8 ▲	*Four Wheel Drive sign. End descent.*
11-10		**N 36° 41.5084' W 112° 2.1291'**
0.3 ▼	8.5 ▼	Historical marker of Expedition 1776.

		19.0▲ Historical marker of Expedition 1776.
11-11		**N 36° 41.5041' W 112° 2.4516'**
1.9 ▼	8.8▼	Rocky, steep ascent.
		18.7▲ Rocky, steep descent.
11-12		**N 36° 42.0781' W 112° 3.9928'**
1.2 ▼	10.7▼	FR 284C straight ahead.
		16.8▲ FR 284C straight ahead.
11-13		**N 36° 42.0967' W 112° 4.9353'**
3.8 ▼	11.9▼	Pass water tank on left. Follow road to the left.
		15.6▲ Keep right, then straight up hill. Water tank on right.
11-14		**N 36° 39.6132' W 112° 5.5718'**
1.7 ▼	15.7▼	Go to right over cattle guard then left on FR 284 (marked FR 224).
		11.8▲ Go to right over cattle guard then left on FR 284C.
11-15		**N 36° 38.6148' W 112° 6.8279'**
0.1 ▼	17.4▼	Cross FR 220 and onto FR 224.
		10.1▲ Cross FR 220 straight onto FR 284.
11-16		**N 36° 38.5883' W 112° 6.8646'**
0.5▼	17.5▼	Steep road next 5.5 miles.
		10.0▲ Steep road ends.
11-17		**N 36° 38.4555' W 112° 7.3615'**
1.7 ▼	18.0▼	Fallen trees throughout area.
		9.5▲ Fallen trees throughout area.
11-18		**N 36° 38.8816' W 112° 9.0753'**
0.5 ▼	19.7▼	Go straight.
		7.8▲ Bear right.
11-19		**N 36° 38.9569' W 112° 9.5706'**
0.2 ▼	20.2▼	Bear left,
		7.3▲ FR 224A on left. Right for GWT.

11-20			**N 36° 38.8809' W 112° 9.6779'**
0.2 ▼	20.4 ▼		End steep road.
		7.1 ▲	*Steep road next 5.5 miles.*
11-21			**N 36° 38.9734' W 112° 9.8447'**
0.5 ▼	20.6 ▼		Turn right onto FR 225.
		6.9 ▲	*Turn left onto FR 224.*
11-22			**N 36° 39.4096' W 112° 9.7718'**
0.9 ▼	21.1 ▼		FR205 on left. Go straight on FR 225.
		6.4 ▲	*Go straight ahead onto FR 255.*
11-23			**N 36° 40.1226' W 112° 9.5843'**
3.4 ▼	22.0 ▼		Stay on FR 225. FR 205B on left.
		5.5 ▲	*Stay on FR 225. FR 205B on right.*
11-24			**N 36° 42.5574' W 112° 10.2592'**
0.4 ▼	25.4 ▼		Bear right. Campground off to left.
		2.1 ▲	*Bear left. Campground off to right.*
11-25			**N 36° 42.6365' W 112° 9.9086'**
0.1 ▼	25.8 ▼		Turn left on FR 225.
		1.7 ▲	*FR 225A straight ahead. Turn right on FR 225.*
11-26			**N 36° 42.6715' W 112° 10.0545'**
1.6 ▼	25.9 ▼		Go straight on FR 225. FR 258B is on the left.
		1.6 ▲	*Go straight on FR 225. FR 258B is on the right.*
11-27			**N 36° 43.9711' W 112° 10.5059'**
Arrive	27.5 ▼		Exit at US 89A. Turn left for Jacob Lake, right for Marble Canyon.
		0.0 ▲	*Turn south from US 89A onto FR 225 at milepost 576.*

11-1: Entry to House Rock.

11-9: Warning Sign.

11-10: Historical Marker

11-17: Fallen Tree Area

11-11: Long Descent to House Rock

Great Western Trail 12:
Jacob Lake to Utah

This last leg of the Great Western Trail lies in the Arizona Strip, which is red-rock canyon country north of the Colorado River. Sagebrush predominates in the lower elevations; juniper, piñon, Ponderosa pines, fir, aspen and spruce forests replace it in the upper elevations.

The area, settled by Jacob Hamblin and the Mormon Pioneers in the 1800s, has been the last stronghold of polygamy, even though the Mormon Church banned the practice in 1890. Navajo parties often raided the Mormon settlements until Hamblin forged a peace treaty with them.

Two Spanish priests, Dominguez and Escalante, in the late 1700s had opened the Jacob Hamblin Road, but it was unused for years until a friendly Paiute showed Hamblin the steep, rocky trail. Members of the Mormon Church from Arizona used this trail, which went from the Echo Cliffs along present-day US 89, across the Colorado River at Lees Ferry, and then along the Vermilion Cliffs, to get to the temple of St. George in Utah. There they sealed their marriage before beginning their long, difficult journey home. Because of the numbers of couples who made the trip, the trail became known as the "Honeymoon Trail."

How to Get There:

To Waypoint 1: From Arizona, US 89A, turn north onto FR 257 at milepost 576.

To Waypoint 26: From Utah, US 89, turn south onto Road 730, between mileposts 43 and 44.

Roads comprising trail:

From US 89A in Arizona: FR 257 – FR 249 – FR 247 – FR 248 – FR 248A – FR 248AA - BLM 1024 - Mormon Honeymoon

Trail - Jacob Hamblin Road.

In Utah: Road 715 - Kane County Road K4000 (also Road 715) - Road 720 - Road 730 .

Open months/Best Travel: Mid-May to November. This trail may close in the winter because of snow and rainy conditions. Contact the North Kaibab Ranger District or the Bureau of Land Management before embarking on your trip.

Permits: None required in Arizona. You will need a free permit to overnight backpack or car camp if you enter the trail from Utah. They are in a metal lectern in the parking area at the entrance to the trail.

Elevation Min/Max: 5339'/7674'

Paved Mileage: none.

Unpaved Mileage: 31.4 miles.

Travel Time: 3 hours 30 minutes.

Difficulty: Most of the trail is easy to moderate, however the steep descent and narrow switchbacks at waypoint 17 require careful wheel placement and expert driving skill.

Remoteness: 4/4

Services Available: none on the trail. Fuel and services are available at Jacob Lake and Marble Canyon in Arizona, or at Kanab, in Utah.

Driving the Trail: Begin the trail at mile marker 579, 2.7 miles south of Jacob Lake on US 89-Alt. Turn north onto FR 257. The trail in this heavily forested area is mostly gravel without obstacles. At waypoint 5 you enter Orderville Canyon, which according to an interpretive sign in the area, "was named after the Orderville United Order, a Mormon Church cooperative which established a dairy and sheep ranching operation in the canyon around 1880."

Further on you will enter the grasslands of Summit Valley and the Willis Canyon Allotment (waypoint 7). The Arizona Trail is about 30 yards to the right of the sign.

The Navajo Trail crosses the GWT just past waypoint 7. According to one source, this is an old Indian and shepherding trail; according to the interpretive sign on the trail, it was a Paiute Indian Trail used by the Navajos during the Navajo Indian Wars. This trail is closed to motor vehicles.

The road gets rougher at waypoint 9. You get a breathtaking

view of the Vermilion Cliffs from the Buckskin Mountains at waypoint 17 (cover photograph) before beginning a steep, winding descent down the Mormon Honeymoon Trail and the Jacob Hamblin Road at waypoint 19.

The trail becomes easy again from this point. At waypoint 20 you cross into Utah on an easy but rutted and bumpy road. At waypoint 26 the trail ends, and with it your journey on the Great Western Trail in Arizona.

Congratulations! We hope you enjoyed it.

At the exit turn left for Kanab and Arizona or cross the highway to begin the Utah section of the Great Western Trail which we do not describe in this book.

Trail Information: North Kaibab Ranger District, Bureau of Land Management (Appendix B).

Restrictions: Information regarding the use of the Jacob Lake Campground, Jacob Lake Group Camping Area, Demotte Campground, and the Indian Hollow campground are available from the North Kaibab Ranger District.

Map References:

USGS:

1:24,000: Jacob Lake, Cooper Ridge, Buck Pasture Canyon, Petrified Hollow.

1:100,000: Fredonia (AZ), Kanab (UT).

1:250,000: Grand Canyon (AZ), Cedar City (UT)

Terrain Navigator DVD: Arizona North (AZ9)

Arizona Road & Recreation Atlas: p. 28, 62.

USDA Forest Service Map: Kaibab National Forest, North Kaibab Ranger District; Great Western Trail Kaibab National Forest.

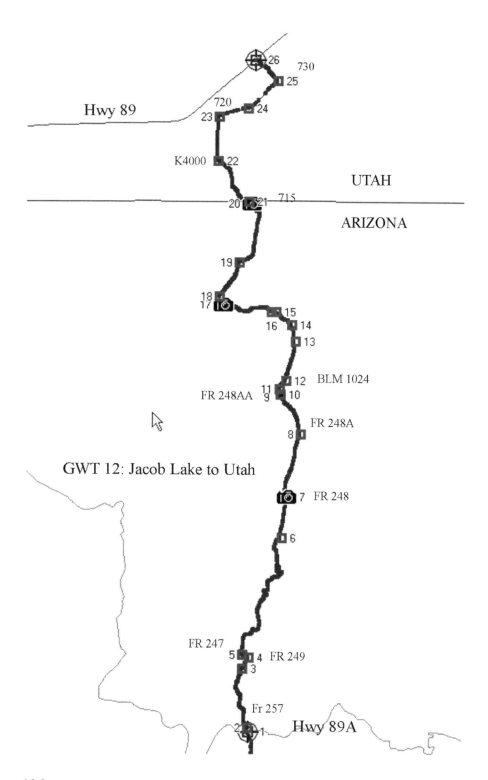

Hwy 89

720
23

K4000 22

UTAH

20 21 715

ARIZONA

19

18
17

15
16 14

13

12 BLM 1024

FR 248AA 11
9 10

FR 248A

8

GWT 12: Jacob Lake to Utah

7 FR 248

6

FR 247

5 4 FR 249
3

Fr 257

2 1 Hwy 89A

106

GWT 12: Jacob Lake to Utah

12-1		**N 36° 43.9770' W 112° 10.5177'**
0.2 ▼	0.0▼	From US 89A, milepost 576, turn north onto FR 257.
	31.4▲	*Exit at US 89A. Straight to GWT 11, turn right for Jacob Lake.*
12-2		**N 36° 44.1232' W 112° 10.5360'**
2.3 ▼	0.2▼	FR 487 on right. Go straight.
	31.2▲	*FR 487 on left. Go straight.*
12-3		**N 36° 45.9044' W 112° 10.7457'**
0.5 ▼	2.5▼	FR 290 on left. Bear right.
	28.9▲	*FR 290 on right. Bear left.*
12-4		**N 36° 46.2292' W 112° 10.4940'**
0.3 ▼	3.0▼	Bear left onto FR 249.
	28.4▲	*Turn right onto FR 257*
12-5		**N 36° 46.3271' W 112° 10.7524'**
5.5 ▼	3.3▼	Turn right at cattle guard onto FR 247.
	28.1▲	*Turn left after cattle guard onto FR 249.*
12-6		**N 36° 49.8656' W 112° 9.2946'**
1.4 ▼	8.8▼	Willis Canyon Allotment. Arizona Trail on right.
	22.6▲	*Willis Canyon Allotment. Arizona Trail on left.*
12-7		**N 36° 51.1039' W 112° 9.1165'**
2.3 ▼	10.2▼	Go straight onto FR 248, then cross Navajo Trail.
	21.2▲	*Continue straight onto FR 247.*
12-8		**N 36° 53.0185' W 112° 8.5844'**
1.5 ▼	12.5▼	Bear left onto FR 248A,
	18.9▲	*Bear right onto FR 248A,*
12-9		**N 36° 54.0933' W 112° 9.2543'**
0.2 ▼	14.0▼	FR 248A on left. Go straight onto FR 248AA. Rough road ahead.

	17.4▲	*FR 248A on right. Straight on FR 248A.*
12-10		**N 36° 54.2067' W 112° 9.3497'**
0.2 ▼	14.2▼	Cattle guard. Leaving Kaibab Forest.
	17.2▲	Cattle guard. Entering Kaibab Forest.
12-11		**N 36° 54.3689' W 112° 9.3842'**
0.4 ▼	14.4▼	Bear right.
	17.0▲	*Bear left.*
12-12		**N 36° 54.6295' W 112° 9.1538'**
1.4 ▼	14.8▼	Cross BLM Road 1025 onto BLM Road 1024 straight ahead.
	16.6▲	*Cross BLM Road 1025. Go straight.*
12-13		**N 36° 55.8269' W 112° 8.8059'**
0.6 ▼	16.2▼	BLM 1024 straight ahead.
	15.2▲	*Stay on trail.*
12-14		**N 36° 56.3092' W 112° 8.9373'**
0.8 ▼	16.8▼	Straight ahead.
	14.6▲	*Straight ahead.*
12-15		**N 36° 56.7215' W 112° 9.5418'**
0.2 ▼	17.6▼	Bear left.
	13.8▲	*Bear right.*
12-16		**N 36° 56.7071' W 112° 9.7122'**
1.9 ▼	17.8▼	Bear right.
	13.6▲	*Bear left.*
12-17		**N 36° 56.9226' W 112° 11.4998'**
0.4 ▼	19.7▼	Begin steep descent, sharp turns, loose rock.
	11.7▲	*End of steep ascent.*
12-18		**N 36° 57.1794' W 112° 11.6485'**
1.5 ▼	20.1▼	Keep right on Honeymoon Trail.
	11.3▲	*Keep left. Steep ascent ahead.*
12-19		**N 36° 58.2113' W 112° 10.9036'**
2.6 ▼	21.6▼	Turn right onto Jacob Hamblin Road. Honeymoon Trail continues to left.
	9.8▲	*Turn left onto Jacob Hamblin Road.*

12-20		**N 36° 59.9985' W 112° 10.4710'**
0.1 ▼	24.2▼	Utah/Arizona State Line.
	7.2▲	*Utah/Arizona State Line.*
12-21		**N 37° 0.0668' W 112° 10.5564'**
1.9 ▼	24.3▼	Bear left, then straight on Road 715.
	7.1▲	*Bear right after Arizona GWT sign.*
12-22		**N 37° 1.2876' W 112° 11.7066'**
1.6 ▼	26.2▼	Turn right on Kane County road K4000 (also Road 715).
	5.2▲	*Turn left onto Road 715.*
12-23		**N 37° 2.6218' W 112° 11.6907'**
1.0 ▼	27.8▼	Turn right on Road 720.
	3.6▲	*Turn left onto K4000 (also marked Road 715).*
12-24		**N 37° 2.8615' W 112° 10.6220'**
1.4 ▼	28.8▼	Go straight on Road 720.
	2.6▲	*Stay on Road 720.*
12-25		**N 37° 3.6888' W 112° 9.4885'**
1.2 ▼	30.2▼	Turn left onto Road 730.
	1.2▲	*Turn right onto Road 720.*
12-26		**N 37° 4.3253' W 112° 10.3292'**
Arrive	31.4▼	Exit Hwy 89 turn left for US 89A and Arizona.
	0.0▲	*Turn south onto Road 730 from US 89 between mileposts 43 & 44*

Along the trail

12-7: Navajo Trail   12-20: Crossing into Utah

Orderville Canyon   Willis Canyon Allotment

12-17: Vermillion Cliffs from Buckskin Mountain

Great Western Trail 13:
The Navajo Reservation

Despite printed information to the contrary, the Great Western Trail does not travel across the Navajo Reservation, and according to a Ranger who was a member of a commission studying the proposal, will not do so in the future.

We include it as Trail 13 because for a small fee payable at the Ranger Station in Cameron, you can drive across its vast grassland and camp wherever you wish. Camping is primitive, so bring all your necessities with you.

The 360,000 acre Little Colorado River Gorge, which adjoins the eastern boundary of Grand Canyon National Park, became a Navajo Tribal Park in 1962. You can enter it from Highway 64 and may buy jewelry, pottery and other items from Navajo vendors who have set up stands along the highway.

Cameron, a Navajo Trading Post on route 89, is well worth a visit. Food, lodging, and services are available here and at the junction of Highways 89 and 64.

While driving on the reservation you will see hogans, the traditional Navajo log, brush and mud house with five, six or eight sides (photo p. 95). Its entrance always faces the rising sun. Most Navajo today live in modern houses, but some still live in hogans, which are used for family ceremonies.

Open Range rules apply here. Livestock have the right-of-way and you are responsible for any injury you cause them while driving on the reservation.

How to Get There:

To Waypoint 1: The entrance to the reservation is west of Highway 89, approximately 1.1 miles north of The Gap. There are no markers except for a cattle guard, so follow the

GPS coordinates.

Roads Comprising Trail: Indian Land Route 6130, from and to Highway 89. Since this is not part of the Great Western Trail, there is no specific trail to follow. We include the one we drove to the Salt Trail Canyon. Other possibilities are available, and the Navajo Rangers will give you a rudimentary map when you pay for your permit.

Open months/Best Travel: Mid-May to November. There may be thunderstorms in July and August, as well as snow in the winter.

Permits: Permits presently cost $5/day a person with an another $5/person to camp, and are required for all travel and camping on the reservation. You can order them by mail or purchase them at the Navajo Ranger Station in Cameron.

Elevation Min/Max: 5388'/5795'

Mileage: 16.2 miles

Unpaved Mileage: 16.2

Time: 30 minutes.

Difficulty: Easy.

Remoteness Rating: 2/4

Services: none along trail. Snacks and gasoline available at The Gap on Highway 89. Tuba City is nearby.

Driving the Trail: Once past the cattle guard at waypoint 1, bear to the right to leave the housing area and get to open land. The roads are mostly graded and maintained and are marked by improvised sculptures. If you choose to discover your own road to the Salt Trail Canyon, or to explore a different area of the reservation, turn on the "breadcrumb" tracker on your GPS so you will be able to find your way back to the highway.

Road Information: Navajo Ranger Stations and Visitors Centers across the reservation. (Appendix B).

Restrictions: Permits required. No camping in populated areas.

Map References:

USGS:

1:24,000: The Gap, Bodaway Mesa, Pillow Mt, Salt Trail Canyon.

1:100,000: Tuba City

1:250,000: Marble Canyon.

Terrain Navigator: Arizona North (AZ9)

Arizona Road & Recreation Atlas: p. 29, 63.

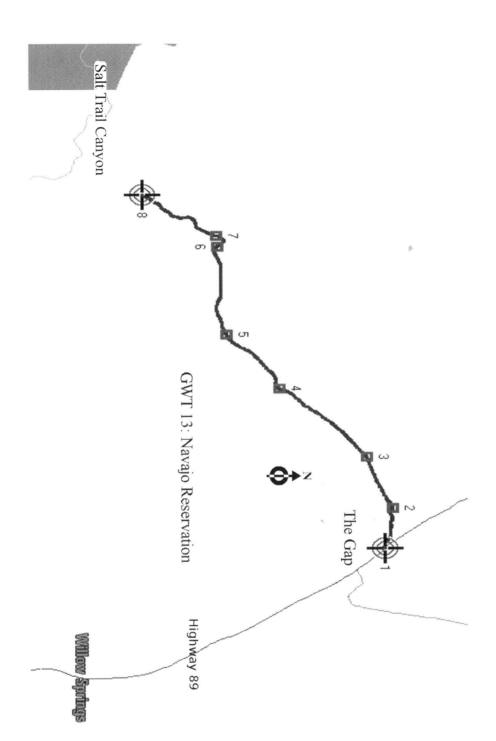

Salt Trail Canyon

GWT 13: Navajo Reservation

N

The Gap

Highway 89

Willow Springs

113

GWT 13: Camping on Indian Lands

13-1		**Arrive**	**N 36° 18.9318' W 111° 28.4198'**
1.5 ▼	0.0 ▼		Enter west of Hwy 89, 1.1 mi north of The Gap.
		16.1 ▲	*Exit onto Hwy 89. Turn left for GWT 11, right for Flagstaff.*
13-2			**N 36° 19.1333' W 111° 29.9398'**
2.0 ▼	1.5 ▼		Keep Hole Reservoir on left.
		14.6 ▲	*Keep Hole Reservoir on right.*
13-3			**N 36° 18.4838' W 111° 31.8808'**
3.5 ▼	3.5 ▼		Go straight.
		12.6 ▲	*Go straight.*
13-4			**N 36° 16.3211' W 111° 34.4471'**
2.5 ▼	6.9 ▼		Bear right.
		9.2 ▲	*Bear left.*
13-5			**N 36° 15.0059' W 111° 36.4855'**
3.2 ▼	9.5 ▼		Go straight.
		6.6 ▲	*Go Straight.*
13-6			**N 36° 14.7808' W 111° 39.8223'**
0.6 ▼	12.7 ▼		Go straight.
		3.4 ▲	*Go straight.*
13-7			**N 36° 14.7642' W 111° 40.2291'**
2.8 ▼	13.3 ▼		Turn left.
		2.8 ▲	*Turn right.*
13-8			**N 36° 12.9206' W 111° 41.7851'**
Arrive	16.1 ▼		Arrive at Salt Trail Canyon.
		0.0 ▲	*Leave Salt Trail Canyon.*

Camping on the Navajo Reservation

Salt Trail Canyon

115

Appendix A: What to bring along.

This list is only a guide; modify it to suit your personal needs. Your vehicle's condition and its quirky needs, the time you intend to travel, the number of people in your party, and your comfort needs all require careful, individual consideration.

Bring what you feel is essential but avoid adding unnecessary weight that may compromise your vehicle's efficiency.

Your primary focus should be water, fuel, and communication devices.

Vehicle equipment:
Fuel.
Consider engine oils (motor, transmission, brake and steering), but don't plan to change your oil and oil filter along the trail.
Shovel, ax, flares.
High lift jack, lug wrench.
Fire extinguisher.
Multitool kit, such as the one available from Harbor Freight (metric sizes for foreign vehicles, SAE otherwise. Bring both for newer trucks).
Sledgehammer, crowbar.
Multimeter.
Fuse, nuts and bolts assortments.
Engine belts (better to check them before you leave home).
Hose clamps, JB Weld.
Tow strap.
Fire extinguisher.
Rags, hand cleaner, electrical and duct tape, zip ties.
Spare tire, valve core, core removing tool and cap, lug nuts, extra set of keys.
Tire plug kit. I do not recommend gunk in a can since it does

not seal punctures in the sidewall of the tire and you must remove it as soon as possible since it will cause tire imbalance.

Maps, GPS, this book.

Tire pressure gauge, bicycle tire pump.

CB, cellphone, ham radio (you don't need a license to use it in an emergency), satellite phone or PLB (personal locator beacon).

Complete pre-trip vehicle inspection.

Tarpaulin to lie on when you're working under your vehicle. You can also use it for shade when you're lost in the desert.

Winch with accessories.

Camping gear:

Tent and groundsheet.

Table and chairs.

Lanterns, flashlights, radio.

Sleeping bag and pad, pillow.

Stove with fuel and lighter (important when there are campfire restrictions).

Pots, pans, paper plates and silverware.

Sealable food containers.

Camp suds, matches, paper towels, and trash bags.

Water, water, and more water.

First aid kit.

Personal items:

Rain gear, hat, hiking boots, knife, and compass.

Jacket, sweater and usual clothing.

Toiletries.

Camera.

Medications.

Water and water purification tablets, bug spray.

Signal mirror, waterproof match case.

Police whistle. Three blasts mean, "help needed."

Appendix B: Forest Service Contacts

Arizona State Office of the Bureau of Land Management:
Jim Kenna, State Director
Ray Suazo, Associate State Director
One North Central Avenue, Suite 800
Phoenix, Arizona 85004-4427
Voice: 602-417-9500
Fax: 602-417-9398
Office Hours: 8 am - 4:30 p.m., M-F

Arizona Strip Field Office
345 East Riverside Drive
St. George, UT 84790-6714
Voice: (435) 688-3200
Fax: (435) 688-3258
E-mail: ASFOWEB_AZ@blm.gov
District Manager: Scott Florence
Field Manager: Lorraine Christian
Hours: 7:45 am – 5:00 p.m., Monday-Friday
10:00 am – 3:00 p.m., Saturday

Grand Canyon-Parashant National Monument
345 East Riverside Drive
St. George, UT 84790-6714
Voice: (435) 688-3200
Fax: (435) 688-3258
Monument Manager: Rosie Pepito, Acting
Hours: 7:45 a.m. – 5:00 p.m., Monday-Friday
10:00 am – 3:00 p.m., Saturday

Vermilion Cliffs National Monument

Linda Price, Monument Manager
345 E. Riverside Drive
St. George, UT 84790-6714
Voice: (435) 688-3200

Hassayampa Field Office
21605 N. 7th Avenue
Phoenix, AZ 85027-2929
Voice: (623) 580-5500
Fax: (623) 580-5580
E-mail: PFOWEB_AZ@blm.gov
District Manager: Angelita Bulletts
Field Manager: Steve Cohn
Hours: 7:30 a.m. – 4:15 p.m., M-F

Agua Fria National Monument
Rem Hawes, Monument Manager
21605 N. 7th Avenue
Phoenix, AZ 85027-2929
Voice: (623) 580-5500

Apache and Sitgeaves National Forests:

http://www.fs.fed.us/r3/asnf/

Supervisor's Office
P.O. Box 640
Springerville, AZ 85938
Voice: (928) 333-4301
TTY: (928) 333-6292
Forest Supervisor: Chris Knopp
Public Affairs Officer: Pam Baltimore

Alpine Ranger District
P.O. Box 469 Alpine, AZ 85920
Voice: (928) 339-5000
TTY: (928) 339-4566

Lakeside Ranger District
2022 W White Mt. Bl.
Lakeside, AZ 85929
Voice: (928) 368-2100
TTY: (928) 368-5088

Springerville Ranger District
P.O. Box 760
Springerville, AZ 85938
Voice: (928) 333-6200
TTY: (928) 333-5397

Arizona State Parks:

http://azstateparks.com/index.html

Arizona State Parks
1300 W. Washington Street
Phoenix, AZ85007
(602) 542-4174

Coronado National Forest:

http://www.fs.fed.us/r3/coronado/

Supervisor's Office
Jim Upchurch, Forest Supervisor
300 W. Congress St.
Tucson, AZ 85701
Voice: (520) 388-8300
Fax: (520) 388-8305
Office Hours: 8:00 a.m. to 4:30 p.m., M-F.
Closed on federal holidays.

Nogales Ranger District
James Copeland, District Ranger
303 Old Tucson Road
Nogales, AZ 85621

Voice: (520) 281-2296
(520) 281-2396 FAX
Office Hours: 8:00 a.m. to 4:30 p.m., M-F. Closed on
federal holidays.

Douglas Ranger District
Bill Edwards, District Ranger
1192 West Saddleview Road
Douglas, AZ 85607
Voice: (520) 364-3468
Fax: (520) 364-6667
Office Hours: 8:00 a.m.-4:30 p.m., M-F.
Closed on federal holidays.

Saffron Ranger District
Kent Elliot, District Ranger
711 14th Avenue, Suite D
Saffron, AZ 85546
Voice: (928) 428-4150
Fax: (928) 428-2393
Office Hours: 8am-4pm, M-F.
Closed on federal holidays.

Sierra Vista Ranger District
Annette Chafes, District Ranger
5990 S. Highway 92
Hereford, AZ 85615
Voice: (520) 378-0311
Fax: (520) 378-0519
Office Hours: 8:00 a.m. to 4:30 p.m., M-F.
Closed on federal holidays.

Santa Catalina Ranger District
Stan Helin, District Ranger
Angela Elam, Deputy District Ranger
5700 N. Serbian Canyon Road
Tucson, AZ 85750
Voice: (520) 749-8700

Fax: (520) 749-7723

Coconino National Forest:

http://www.fs.fed.us/r3/coconino/

Supervisor's Office
1824 S. Thompson St.
Flagstaff, AZ 86001
(928) 527-3600, FAX 527-3620
Office Hours:8:00 a.m. to 4:30 p.m., M-F
Fire Dispatch Emergency: (928) 526-0600

Flagstaff Ranger District
5075 N. Highway 89
Flagstaff, AZ 86004
Voice: (928) 526-0866,
Fax: (928) 527-8288
Office Hours: 8:00 a.m. to 4:30 p.m., M-F.

Mormon Lake office
This office is closed to the public.

Red Rock Ranger District and Visitor Contact Center
P. O. Box 20429
8375 State Route 179,
Sedona, AZ 86341-0429
Voice: (928) 203-7500 or (928) 203-2900
Fax: (928) 203-7539
Administration Office Hours: 8:00 a.m. to 4:30 p.m., M-F.
Visitor Center Hours: 8:00 a.m. to 5:00 p.m., 7 days a week.

Happy Jack Info Center - CLOSED
Mogollon Rim Ranger District
8738 Ranger Road
Happy Jack, AZ 86024
Blue Ridge Office:

Voice: (928) 477-2255
Fax; (928) 527-8282
Office Hours: 7:30 a.m. to 4:00 p.m., M-F.

Kaibab National Forest:

http://www.fs.fed.us/
Select Kaibab from Find a Forest or Grassland by Name.

Supervisor's Office
800 South Sixth Street
Williams, AZ 86046
Voice: (928) 635-8200
Fax: (928) 635-8208

Williams Ranger District
742 South Clover Road
Williams, Arizona 86046
Voice: (928) 635-5600
Fax: (928) 635-5680

Williams/Forest Service Visitor Center
Voice: (928) 635-4707

North Kaibab Ranger District
430 South Main Street
PO Box 248
Fredonia, Arizona 86022
Voice: (928) 643-7395
Fax: (928) 643-8105

Kaibab Plateau Visitor Center
Voice: (928) 643-7298

Tusayan Ranger District
176 Lincoln Log Loop
PO Box 3088
Grand Canyon, AZ 86023

Voice: (928) 638-2443
Fax: (928) 638-1065

Navajo Ranger Stations:

http://www.navajonationparks.org/

The Ranger Station closest to the Great Western Trail is the
Cameron Visitor Center
P.O. Box 459
Cameron, AZ 86020
Voice: (928) 679-2303
Fax: (928) 679-2017
email: lcr@navajonationparks.org
This is located on the southwest corner of the intersection of
Highways 89 and 64.

Prescott National Forest:

http://www.fs.fed.us/r3/prescott/

Supervisor's Office
344 S Cortez Street
Prescott AZ 86303
Voice: (928) 443-8000
TTY: (928) 443-8001
Email: Debbie Maneely: dmaneely@fs.fed.us

Bradshaw Ranger District
44 S Cortez St
Prescott AZ 86303
Voice: (928) 443-8000
TTY: (928) 443-8001

Chino Valley Ranger District
735 N Highway 89
Chino Valley, AZ 86323
Voice: (928) 777-2200

TTY: (928) 443-8001

Verde Ranger District
P.O. Box 670
300 East Highway 260
Camp Verde, AZ 86322
Voice: (928) 567-4121
TTY: (928) 443-8001

Prescott Fire Center
2400 Melville Road
Prescott AZ 86301
Voice: (928) 777-5610
TTY: (928) 443-8001

Tonto National Forest:

http://www.fs.fed.us/
Select Tonto from Find a Forest or Grassland by Name.

Supervisor's Office
2324 E. McDowell Road
Phoenix, Arizona 85006
Voice: (602) 225-5200

Cave Creek Ranger District
40202 N. Cave Creek Road
Scottsdale, AZ 85262
Voice: (480) 595-3300

Globe Ranger District
7680 S. Six Shooter Canyon Road
Globe, Arizona 85501
Voice: (928) 402-6200

Mesa Ranger District
5140 E. Ingram Street.
Mesa, Arizona 85205

Voice: (480) 610-3300

Usery Mountain Park Recreation Area
Voice: (480) 984-0032

Payson Ranger District
1009 E. Hwy 260
Payson, Arizona 85541
Voice: (928) 474-7900

Pleasant Valley Ranger District
P.O. Box 450, FR 63
Young, Arizona 85554
Voice: (928) 462-4300

Tonto Basin Ranger District
28079 N. AZ Highway 188
Roosevelt, Arizona 85545
Voice: (928) 467-3200

Bibliography

Arizona Road & Recreation Atlas, Benchmark Maps, Medford, Oregon 2010 6th edition, revised 2010.

Barnes, Will C. Arizona Place Names. Tucson: The University of Arizona Press, 1988.

Blair, Gerry. Rockhounding Arizona. Falcon Press Publishing Co. Inc, 1997.

Blumberg, George P. "Driving: Going Off Road, Two by Two," The New York Times, www.nytimes.com, 19 Dec. 2003.

Chronic, Halka. Roadside Geology of Arizona. Mountain Press Publishing Company, Missoula, MT. 1995.

Green, Stewart. Arizona Scenic Drives. Falcon Press Publishing Co. Inc, 1992.

"Quick Tips for Responsible Four Wheeling." Tread Lightly!. http://www.treadlightly.org/files_text/4x4_tips_sm.pdf (accessed 7 February 2011).

Trimble, Marshall. Arizona A Cavalcade of History. Treasure Chest Publications, Tucson, Arizona, 1989.

USDA Forest Service Map, Kaibab National Forest, North Kaibab Ranger District, 1994, Revised 2003, 2006.

USDA Forest Service Map, Kaibab National Forest, Williams and Tusayan Ranger Districts, 1995, Revised 2003.

USDA Forest Service Map, Motor Vehicle Use Map, Prescott National Forest 01 Aug 2009.

USDA Forest Service Map, Prescott National Forest, 1993, revised 2000.

USDA Forest Service Map, Tonto National Forest, Arizona 2001.

US Department of the Interior Bureau of Land Management, Dispersed Camping.

The Authors

Raymond and Jennifer Andrews have been avid off-road enthusiasts since 1997 when they first began exploring the desert around Winslow, Arizona. By 1999 they had driven all of the easier trails in the Phoenix area and were looking for new challenges and a new vehicle. They found the first on the Rubicon Trail, one of the most notorious and difficult trails in the country. Under the expert tutelage of Harald Pietschmann, owner of the Adventure Company, they learned to drive over boulders as high as the hood of a Jeep and to avoid mistakes that could result in a rollover or costly vehicle repair.

The second was a new yellow Jeep they modified to face and survive the toughest off-road challenges Arizona has to offer.

A year after their trip to the Rubicon they were featured in an article in The New York Times, "Going off Road, Two by Two," by George P. Blumberg.

Since then they have gone on numerous trips into the wilderness in Arizona and California with their Jeep and trailers. This book details the challenges they encountered and the roads they traveled while mapping and driving the Great Western Trail in Arizona.

Made in the USA
Lexington, KY
27 May 2012